THE
Fruit Garden
DISPLAYED

THE ROYAL HORTICULTURAL SOCIETY
VINCENT SQUARE LONDON SW1

SBN 900629 14 2
© 1974 *The Royal Horticultural Society*
Designed by Peter Newbolt, Cley, Norfolk
Printed in England by
W & J Mackay Limited, Chatham
by Photo-litho
First published 1951
Revised editions 1956, 1965, 1968, 1974, 1978
Reprinted 1975

CONTENTS

ACKNOWLEDGEMENTS

The help of many people in preparing this revised edition is gratefully acknowledged, in particular the staff of the Scientific Liaison Section at East Malling Research Station (especially Mr B. Self) and the staff of the R.H.S. Garden (particularly Mr H. Baker the Society's Fruit Officer, and also Mr R. P. Scase). The Society repeats its thanks to all those who helped in the production of earlier editions of the book which form the basis of this revision.

Permission from the following to reproduce photographs is also acknowledged with thanks: East Malling Research Station: The Comptroller of Her Majesty's Stationery Office: Shell.

METRICATION

Metric measurements are included for the first time. These are not exact equivalents but are given as near as possible for practical use.

PLANNING THE FRUIT GARDEN

Probably most gardeners can devote only a modest area of land to a fruit garden and so it is important to make the fullest possible use of the space available. In a new garden some part of it should be marked off for use only for growing fruit. The planting of bushes and trees should be planned and not done in a haphazard way as in so many old gardens. The number of bushes and trees to be planted depends not only on the size of the fruit garden but also on the cultivars selected, on the rootstocks on which the top fruits, i.e. apples, pears, plums and peaches, are grown, and on the form of trees and method of pruning which may be adopted. The main points to be observed are:

1. grouping together of the same kinds of fruit;
2. proportions of the areas to be devoted to soft and tree fruits;
3. rootstocks for the tree fruits;
4. shapes and types of tree and methods of pruning.

By grouping together the same kinds of fruit, spraying is made easier. It is also an advantage to keep together those fruits which have the same manurial requirements. For instance, apples, gooseberries and red currants need plenty of potash, whilst pears, plums and black currants require more nitrogen.

The question of the proportion of soft fruits to tree fruits is largely one of personal taste, but with a very small garden it might be best to grow mainly soft fruits with a single row of apples or pears on dwarfing rootstocks. When possible wall or fence space should also be used.

Large free-growing trees are unsuitable for most small gardens. With cordons, dwarf pyramids and other trained forms of trees which require a restrictive type of pruning, it is possible to grow many more trees in a given area and so obtain a wider variety to spread the season than could be grown if bush trees were planted.

The purchase of good healthy stock is one of the secrets of success. In soft fruits vigour may be considerably reduced through infection with virus diseases and the Ministry of Agriculture has a scheme for inspecting and granting certificates to stocks of disease-free black currants, strawberries and raspberries. Where possible always buy this Certified Stock.

Virus diseases also affect the growth and crop of tree fruits, but in recent years, nurseries have been able to obtain virus-tested cultivars and rootstocks as 'mother' trees which can be used for propagation. Trees of many cultivars of apple, plum, pear and cherry from these healthy sources are now available from some nurserymen.

First in this book come the general principles of fruit-growing, including choice of site, nutrition, pest and disease control, and weed control. The next section covers the kinds of fruit which give the quickest returns, i.e. the soft fruits – strawberries, raspberries, currants, gooseberries and blackberries. The third section covers the tree fruits, which take longer to fruit, namely apples, pears, plums, peaches, cherries and figs. The neglected fruit garden is discussed in the next section: and the final section is a monthly reminder of jobs in the fruit garden.

The diagrams on the next two pages show three demonstration fruit plots suitable for amateurs, planted at the R.H.S. Garden, Wisley; similar ones are planted at East Malling Research Station. Any necessary modifications to suit individual requirements, should not be difficult.

Model fruit gardens

GARDEN NO. 1 (48 ft by 90 ft : 14.5 m. by 27.5 m.) shows how an area sufficiently large for the requirements of a small household could be laid out to give a good selection of hardy fruits.

At the north end of this plot are eight pyramid stone fruit trees, planted 12 ft (3.7 m.) by 12 ft (3.7 m.). These include plums and gages, a damson and a morello cherry. By planting these trees, which are the largest in the garden, at the north end there is no likelihood that they will shade the other fruits. Four rows of cordons are grown which are 60 ft (18 m.) long; two of pears and two of apples, spaced at 2½ ft (0.75 m.) by 6 ft (1.8 m.). The rows run from south to north and the trees are planted at 45°, sloping to the north. The cultivars are arranged

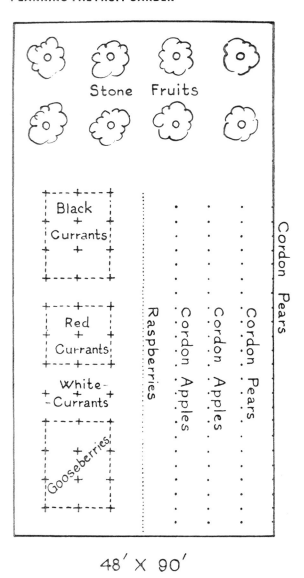

48' X 90'

in sequence of ripening; with apples, for example, the season starts in August with 'Owen Thomas' and ends in March with 'King's Acre Pippin'. The garden contains a 60 ft (18 m.) row of raspberries, blocks of black currants, red currants and gooseberries and a short row of white currants.

GARDEN NO. 2 (48 ft by 60 ft : 14.5 m. × 18 m.) is smaller than Garden No. 1, the main area being devoted to cordon apples and pears. This plot contains five pyramid stone fruit trees planted on the north side. The soft fruits include a row of raspberries and small blocks of black and red currants and gooseberries.

GARDEN NO. 3 (30 ft by 60 ft : 9 m. × 18 m.) is of simple character, suitable for those with limited time for gardening. The bush apples, which are on a dwarfing stock, should require the minimum of attention.

This garden consists largely of bush apples planted at 10 ft (3.1 m.) by 12 ft (3.7 m.), with a row of cordon pears on the east boundary. It also contains a row of raspberries and small groups of black and red currants and gooseberries.

Garden No. 1.

Garden No. 2.

Garden No. 3.

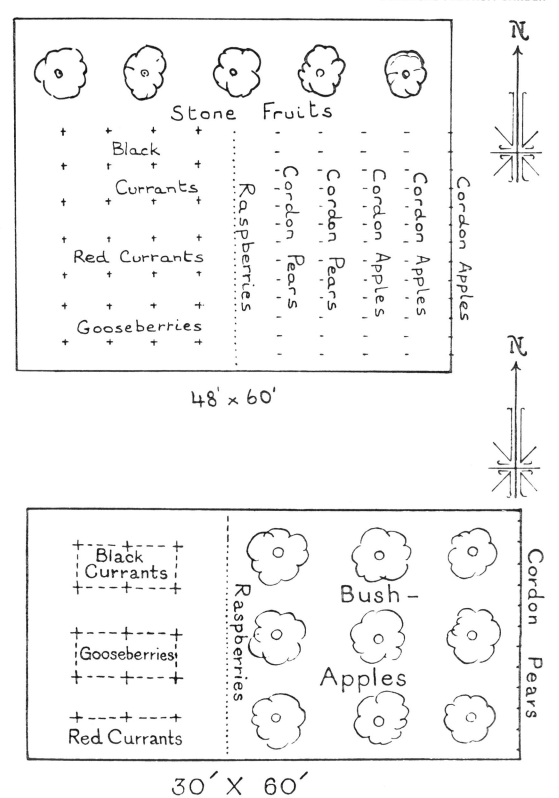

48' × 60'

30' X 60'

GENERAL PRINCIPLES

The amateur fruit-grower has as a rule little choice of soil or even site. He has to accept the soil and site on which his house is built. If, however, he wishes to plan his garden to the best advantage, he must know the conditions that suit the different kinds of fruit. The conditions most favourable for soft fruit are described under each fruit.

Apples, pears, plums and other top fruits can all be grown successfully on many different types of soil, but the ideal one is probably a slightly acid, fairly deep, well-drained, medium loam. Dessert apples, especially 'Cox's Orange Pippin', require the best positions, soils and drainage. Pears are rather less tolerant of very dry conditions than are apples. Plums and cooking apples can be grown satisfactorily in a wider range of soils and conditions. Heavy soils will give good results, provided drainage is good and the ground is well prepared with the subsoil thoroughly broken up. Gravel and chalk soils are not good, but if they are well trenched and plenty of dung or composted material is incorporated with the subsoil, results may be reasonable. Light, dry soils present a problem, but here again generous applications of organic manures or compost before planting will help considerably.

Frost can have a serious effect on fruit. Cold air, being heavier than warmer air, tends to collect in pockets in low-lying ground, particularly in valleys where there is no outlet for it. Such frost pockets should be avoided if possible. It is very difficult to obtain regular crops in such situations without elaborate precautions. Some cultivars of fruits are less prone to frost damage and these are indicated in the lists of recommended cultivars. In the case of cordons and small trees some protection against late spring frosts can be given with sacking, frost proof mats or hessian supported on a framework, but this must be made very secure so that the blossoms or young fruitlets are not damaged.

Preparation of the site

All hardy fruits, with the possible exception of figs, need to have the site deeply dug and thoroughly prepared. With shallow soils it is almost impossible to grow good fruit over a number of years unless the subsoil is well broken up. Deep digging should not be carried out close to the roots of any fruit bushes or trees after planting. Soft fruits are surface rooting and much harm is done by digging too near the roots. The sites must therefore be thoroughly prepared before planting and all perennial weeds removed. The land should be well drained and there should never be stagnant water on the site.

The types of soil which suit individual fruits are referred to in the text; where the soil is not of a type likely to be suitable, efforts should be made to improve it when the ground is first dug and prepared, but no manure should be in contact with the roots at planting.

DIGGING ONE SPIT DEEP

This consists of breaking up the soil to the depth of a spade or a fork. A trench is taken out and the soil from the next strip is turned over into the trench.

If manure is to be applied it is a good plan to spread it over the ground to be dug to ensure even distribution, leaving the breadth of the first spade-cut clear of manure. When the strip has been dug and the soil removed, the manure from the next strip to the width of a spade should be placed in the trench, laying it on the sloping surface. Then the next strip of soil should be turned over into the trench, burying the manure, which is evenly distributed in the soil from the bottom of the trench almost to the surface.

DOUBLE-DIGGING CULTIVATED GROUND

Divide the plot into two, and mark out the boundary and dividing lines with a spade; then take out a trench, 2 feet (60 cm.) wide, and with vertical sides, to the depth of the spade at the end of one half of the plot. The soil should be placed at the same end of the plot, but opposite the other half, where it will be ready to fill in the last trench. Then break up the bottom of the trench to the full depth of a fork. Take care to break up the soil in the middle and the sides of the trench. Next, a second strip of exactly the same width should be marked off, and for this purpose it is a good plan to keep a stick cut to the right length at each side of the ground which is being trenched. Put the line across at the end of your sticks to mark how broad the next trench is to be. Then take out the second trench, placing the soil from it on to the broken-up bottom of the first trench. A trench 2 feet (60 cm.) wide can be conveniently worked in three spits. Each time the first of the three spits to be moved should be the one farthest from the trench which is being filled in, and it should be placed so that it forms a good wall to the second trench. Then the second and third spits may be removed. The second trench, like the first, should be to the full depth of a spade before the bottom is broken up. To do this, it will be necessary to remove the 'crumbs' from the

The model fruit garden at Wisley.

second trench with a shovel. When this has been done, the bottom of the second trench is broken up with a fork, and filled with the soil from the third and so on.

When manure is to be applied in double-digging, it should be spread over the broken-up bottom of the trench, and forked into the loose soil there. The manure may be spread over the ground in the same way as for single-digging, but each time before a top strip of soil is moved into the trench the manure is transferred to the broken-up bottom of the trench.

Nutrition

Manuring is an important means of ensuring the healthy growth of fruit plants and of regulating vegetative growth, fruit yield and quality. Each kind of fruit has its own requirements for manures and what is best for plums and black currants will not give the best results for apples, goose-berries and strawberries. This

section deals with general principles only and should be read in conjunction with the special recommendations for individual crops in their respective chapters.

The main manures for fruits contain nitrogen, phosphate and potash. Potash is of outstanding importance for all fruits, phosphates are not so important for the tree fruits and the needs for nitrogen vary. For example, plums and black currants benefit from heavy dressings of nitrogen, but generous nitrogenous manuring for apples, raspberries and strawberries may make the plants over-vegetative and reduce yield and fruit quality.

A balance must be kept between shoot growth and fruiting, with the aim of obtaining heavy crops of good quality for successive years. This can only be achieved by careful manuring, combined with other management practices, and in particular by the prevention of mineral deficiencies and excesses.

No fruits are real lime-loving plants, not even the stone fruits. Most prefer slightly acid soil conditions,* or soils with only small supplies of free lime in them, whilst some fruits will grow well on strongly acid soils provided they are well manured. The great danger from overliming arises in the fact that fruit crops are very susceptible to deficiencies of the so-called trace elements, particularly iron and manganese, and in a soil of high lime content these two elements may become unavailable to the plant.

A first principle in growing fruits should be to avoid highly calcareous soils and to be sparing in applying lime. Lime should only be applied if the soil is very acid.

The second point to stress is the importance of organic matter in fruit soils. Fruit plants must have a free-rooting medium for healthy growth and longevity, and this can be assured only by maintaining a good content of organic matter. For tree fruits such as apples and pears, this may be best achieved by growing the trees in grass after the first 3 or 4 years in clean cultivation, or by dressings of bulky composts or manures used as surface mulches. The grass and other organic materials must be kept clear of the tree trunk. For soft fruits the usual method is to dig in bulky manures or compost before planting.

It is usually necessary to use concentrated organic manures or inorganic fertilisers in addition to bulky manures to supply the right amount of nutrients needed. Any of the usual manures and fertilisers used for other crops are suitable, though a few precautions are necessary in some cases to avoid injury. All chloride-

* The acidity of a soil is measured by pH, a symbol often used in gardening books. A neutral soil has a pH of 7, acid soils have one below and alkaline ones have a reading above 7. The pH of soils can be measured using one of the soil kits on the market.

containing fertilisers, such as muriate of potash, should be used with caution, or not at all, on soft fruits, particularly red currants. Manures and fertilisers should be applied to the soil, and late winter and early spring – February and March – are the best times to apply them.

Excessive manuring, especially with nitrogen, is shown by over-vigorous growth, large dark green leaves, poor fruiting or large, poor-quality fruits.

MINERAL DEFICIENCIES
One of the most useful ways of judging the nutritional status of fruit trees is to become familiar with the signs of different mineral deficiencies. The most important of these are as follows:

Nitrogen: shoot growth poor; shoots thin; leaves small, pale green developing autumn tints of reds and yellows; much bare wood, bark tends to be reddish brown; fruit spurs weak and blossoms tend to be sparse; fruits small and highly coloured. This deficiency is most common in neglected grassed orchards.

Phosphorus: growth characters as for nitrogen and blossoming also sparse; leaves may be dull green and autumn tints purplish or bronze in colour; fruits small, green, with dull flush, and often acid or unpleasant flavour. Symptoms such as these may develop in July and August on trees growing in heavy calcareous clay soils.

Potassium: shoots short, tending to die back, this condition extending to whole branches; leaves may be bluish green or slightly chlorotic and the edges die and become brown giving the condition known as 'marginal leaf scorch'; blossoming may be fairly profuse but the fruitlets mostly drop and those remaining are small, generally of immature appearance, and may be woody or sweet (lacking acid) to taste.

Although these specific deficiencies may occur separately, old trees which have not been fed are more likely to suffer from defici-

encies of both nitrogen and potassium and perhaps also of phosphorus. In these circumstances it is best to correct all these deficiencies by applying a compound fertiliser. Applications of a foliar feed during the growing period are also beneficial to trees which have been neglected or have suffered from faulty root action as a result of drought or water-logging.

Magnesium: after midsummer leaves generally show obvious symptoms, the older leaves becoming chlorotic between the veins, and either the central portions or the marginal areas developing patches of dead tissue. After these symptoms have developed defoliation is sudden and severe. The fruits on such trees may remain small, immature and woody. This trouble can occur as a result of over-manuring with potash but deficiency symptoms may also develop in wet seasons particularly on light soils. It can be corrected by applying magnesium sulphate either as a dressing to the soil in the spring at the rate of one ounce to the square yard (33 g/m²), or as a foliar spray using a 2% solution starting at petal-fall and repeating two or three times at fortnightly intervals.

Iron: shoot growth restricted; leaves at tips of shoots develop yellowing between the veins or become entirely bleached so that no veins show, followed by marginal leaf scorch; branches die back; fruits have pale ground colour but are highly flushed.

Iron deficiency is induced by alkaline conditions, so it occurs on soils which have a high pH, i.e. calcareous soils, and the trouble is therefore often called lime-induced chlorosis. It can be corrected by applying iron in a chelated or fritted form; in both types of compound, the chemical structure is such that the iron they contain can be absorbed by plants, and is not locked up in the soil by chemical reaction.

Iron chelates can be applied as foliage sprays and are quick acting but a soil application in January is usually recommended. Fritted trace elements can only be applied to the soil. In using these compounds, the makers' instructions should be strictly followed in regard to strength of spray, rate of soil dressing and method of application, since the various proprietary products differ in formulation, and particular compounds and methods of application are recommended for special purposes and soil conditions.

Calcium: the effects of this deficiency in the field are likely to be complicated with other symptoms associated with strongly acid soils and may be masked by

Four types of sprayer. Left sprayer with a double action hand pumping mechanism; centre one powered by a hand pump; right another hand sprayer primed after filling by pumping to the correct pressure; below, a syringe which is useful when a small amount of spray is to be supplied.

deficiency symptoms of potassium and magnesium which are usually also in poor supply where calcium is deficient. When the deficiency is severe, however, shoot growth is poor, the tips die and leaves show marginal scorching. Whilst these effects are only likely to be observed on soils of very low calcium content, there is a special condition of the deficiency shown only in apple fruits and which is called bitter pit (see p. 77). This may occur even on highly calcareous soils such as the chalk soils.

Other minerals: deficiency of *manganese* results in chlorosis and die-back; of *zinc*, in the development of very small narrow leaves which occur as 'rosettes' on the end of shoots; of *copper*, in severe die-back of young shoots. These troubles can be corrected by spraying the foliage with solutions of manganese, zinc or copper sulphates respectively. Expert advice should be obtained before applying treatments for these deficiencies.

Pest and Disease Control

Proper preparation of the ground, careful planting and pruning and manuring are of great importance but these measures alone will not always ensure success. If healthy growth and high-quality fruit are to be obtained the major pests and diseases will have to be controlled.

Most pest and disease control on fruit is achieved by applying chemicals, and regular fruit-spraying programmes are widely used in commercial orchards. Amateurs who adopt such spray programmes can obtain dramatic improvements in the production of clean fruit but may also experience further problems, such as a pest developing a resistant strain, or the sudden increase of previously unimportant species when its natural predators and parasites are killed. In addition, it is often difficult to apply sprays thoroughly to large trees and inefficient applications of chemicals are wasteful and can be harmful. If undesirable side-effects are to be

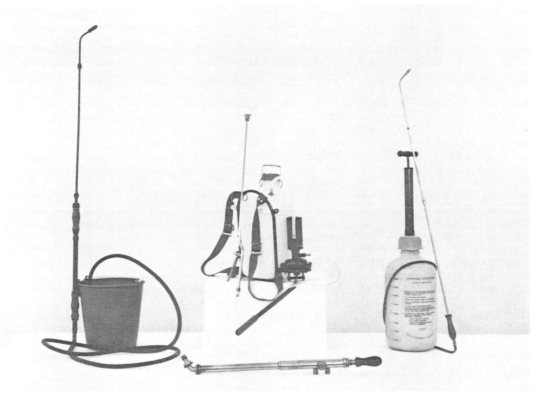

avoided, chemicals should be applied only when there is a real need and instructions for their use must be strictly observed. In particular a minimum interval must elapse between the last application of certain chemicals and picking and using the fruit. The length of these periods ranges from 1 day to 1 month: read the manufacturer's instructions on the label. The use of insecticides, fungicides, herbicides and other crop protection chemicals approved for amateur use under the Ministry of Agriculture's Agricultural Chemicals Approval Scheme is recommended when they are available. Packs of these products can be identified by the sign, a capital A surmounted by a crown, which is always present somewhere on the label.

Insecticides, fungicides and herbicides should always be handled carefully and stored safely out of reach of children and away from foods. Do not spray during blossoming as this will kill hive bees and other pollinators, and avoid any possible drift of chemicals onto adjacent crops, such as vegetables, growing near treated fruit trees.

The best conditions for spraying are when it is dry, calm and frost-free. It is necessary to spray on a dry day as the foliage or bark is then also dry and the solution will stick to it. There are very few days when it is completely calm, however, but spraying can be done when there is a light breeze, provided some arrangements are made to screen adjacent plants, for instance with plastic sheets, if the spray is likely to harm other plants. The spray should be applied from all sides of the plant to give as good a coverage as possible.

Wash thoroughly after spraying and clean spray equipment thoroughly. *Never* use a sprayer that has been used for applying weedkiller as minute traces left in a sprayer can cause severe damage to shoots and foliage.

Thorough spraying of small

Gooseberry shoots showing typical bird damage.

bushes and trees should not be difficult and one of the many hand or pressure sprayers now available should prove adequate. Some of these can be fitted with extension lances to spray larger trees but if many such trees are to be sprayed, some form of motorised sprayer will be needed. Such sprayers are relatively expensive and they are seldom bought by amateur fruit-growers.

In addition to the chemical methods, various non-chemical methods may also be used to reduce the incidence of pests and diseases. Good garden-hygiene and thorough cultivation can limit the spread of some pests and diseases; barriers and traps can be used against pests such as winter moths and codling moth, and it may even be possible to practise some measure of biological control of glasshouse red spider mite on strawberries or woolly aphid on apple.

BIRD DAMAGE TO FRUIT BUDS
Bird damage to overwintering fruit buds can be devastating. The bullfinch is the chief culprit but tits and sparrows are also troublesome. The damage can affect cropping capacity permanently since much of the wood, devoid of any buds, remains blind and unproductive.

The only known effective control is to net over trees and bushes between November and March. Numerous spray materials have been tried but any protection they give does not seem to be consistently reliable, neither are they always available to the amateur.

Scaring devices are many and varied and may give protection for short periods. Experiments have shown that scarers should be used irregularly rather than continuously and their siting should be varied so that birds are less likely to get accustomed to them.

Plum shoot with unproductive wood where birds have stripped off the buds.

Chemical Weed Control

There are a number of herbicides (weedkillers) available to the amateur grower, which can be used in the fruit garden. The correct use of these chemicals can lessen considerably the labour of weed control; in addition the consequent reduction in soil cultivation benefits the fruit plants in that their roots are able to penetrate without disturbance to the more fertile top layer of the soil.

However, there are risks. These can be reduced by:

1. Keeping the chemicals in their *labelled* container, out of the reach of children.
2. Always reading the label carefully before use, using the recommended doses and observing the safety precautions stated.
3. Applying the spray accurately. Calibrate the sprayer using water at first to find out exactly what volume is used over what area.
4. Avoiding spray drift and taking care to prevent contamination of any water source.
5. Washing out the sprayer and the mixing-containers thoroughly before and after use.

Simple weed-killing programmes based on paraquat, simazine, dalapon and dichlobenil are given as an appendix (see pp. 15–16). These four chemicals should be sufficient for the needs of amateur fruit-growers and are available in retail quantities. However, fruit-growers with larger areas may be interested to know that there are other useful herbicides available in commercial quantities, particularly those dealing with specific weed problems or weeds resistant to the chemicals mentioned.

Before any herbicide is used its mode of action should be understood. Inefficient application of chemicals will not give effective weed-control, may cause considerable damage to the crop and render the soil sterile for a long period.

Paraquat will kill any green tissue (green bark, green buds or leaves) on contact. It has a burning or scorching action and should be directed onto the weeds but must be kept clear of the fruit plants. However, dormant woody plants will not be harmed if they are accidentally wetted provided the buds are closed and not green. Paraquat will kill annual weeds and perennial weeds that have no underground food reserves. Perennials such as couch grass, thistle and perennial nettles which have an underground food reserve can be weakened and eventually killed by repeated applications. The chemical is quickly inactivated on reaching the ground on soils containing clay, and so there is no absorption by the roots. However on sandy soils there is a risk of the chemical reaching the roots and damaging them and on such soils care should be taken to wet the soil as little as possible. Paraquat is useful for cleaning up weedy patches at any time of the year by carefully directed applications. In hot weather paraquat quickly takes effect but it is more efficient in cool, dull conditions. In winter the dose of paraquat can usually be reduced by half.

Simazine is a herbicide applied to the soil, and is taken up by germinating weed seeds through their underground or aerial parts before emergence from the soil. It will not kill weed seedlings that have already emerged, nor established weeds. Simazine is used to keep clean land free from weeds in newly planted and established crops of apples, pears, black currants, gooseberries and cane fruits. It can also be used on strawberries at certain times of the year. This herbicide creates a seal or barrier to germinating seeds over the surface of the soil and the best results are obtained by applying it when the soil is moist, firm and has a fine tilth. If the soil is dry when the spray is applied distribution will be poor. As simazine is nearly insoluble in water the spray mixture should be agitated frequently during spraying to prevent the settling out of the powder. Again, because of this insolubility simazine moves downwards very slowly after application, nevertheless on light sandy soils there is the risk of the chemical being washed down onto the roots of the fruit plants and damage may result. It is extremely important to observe the manufacturer's recommendations as to the rate of application, which should be varied according to whether the soil is light, medium or heavy. Simazine is persistent in the soil; the degree of persistence depends on the soil type and the amount applied, but generally seven months at least must elapse before crops grown from seed can be sown in simazine-treated soil.

Overdosing can render the soil sterile for a much longer period. Simazine is applied as an overall spray, the established fruit-plants if wetted will not be harmed provided the recommended dosage is used.

Dalapon is a foliage-applied herbicide which is absorbed into the plant through the leaves, then being distributed within it, and finally killing the plant. It is used for the control of couch, other perennial grasses and annual grasses around apples and pears established for at least four years. There are limitations to its use on certain cultivars, notably 'Cox's Orange Pippin'. It is also used in dormant black currant and gooseberry plantations. Dalapon has only a short term residual effect, generally six to eight weeks, though it may be longer in cold conditions. It is readily taken up by tree or bush roots and applications must be confined to the grass itself using only sufficient spray to wet the foliage without causing excessive run-off. Avoid spraying bare ground. Dalapon is not recommended for stone fruits.

Dichlobenil is a granular herbicide applied to the soil surface, and is useful against existing annual and many perennial weeds in established apple, pear, bush and cane fruit plantations. It also persists for up to 6 months in the soil to give residual control of germinating weed seedlings. Woody weeds such as brambles are resistant.

Adhere to the manufacturer's recommendations. Overdosing, as well as application at the wrong time can lead to serious damage. Keep the material out of water courses.

APPENDIX: HERBICIDES RECOMMENDED

Time of application	Weeds controlled	Chemical name	Notes
Apples and Pears			
Before weeds appear	Nearly all weeds in germinating stage	Simazine	Apply to bare, moist soil, preferably in February or March. In the case of newly planted trees the soil must be well firmed before treatment.
After weeds appear	Annual weeds and shallow-rooted perennials	Paraquat	Use as a directed spray onto weeds at any time of year. Repeated treatments will kill perennials. Paraquat will not penetrate mature bark but avoid spraying the stems of trees less than 3 years old.
When the grass is actively growing in early spring or autumn.	Grass weeds including couch	Dalapon	Use as a directed spray among trees established for at least 4 years. Spray the grass but avoid excessive spray run-off onto soil.
March or early April	Annuals and many perennials including grass	Dichlobenil	Distribute evenly over the soil surface. Do not apply under trees within 2 years of planting.
Gooseberries and Black, Red & White Currants			
Before weeds appear	Nearly all weeds in germinating stage	Simazine	Apply to clean, moist soil, preferably in February or March.
After weeds appear	Annual weeds and shallow rooted perennials	Paraquat	Use as a directed spray on to weeds at any time of the year. Avoid wetting foliage of bushes and the buds of black currant at any time otherwise damage will result.
March or early April	Annuals and many perennials including grass	Dichlobenil	Do not apply to bushes within 2 years of planting or the first year of cropping whichever is the later. Application should not be made to black currants at

Time of application	Weeds controlled	Chemical name	Notes
			any age which have been cut down to soil level until at least 1 year has elapsed after cutting back. Ensure the granules do not lodge within the buds and leaves.
Between leaf fall and end of December	Grass weeds including partial control of couch	Dalapon	Apply as a directed spray onto the grass but avoid excessive spray run-off onto soil. Use among bushes planted out for at least one year.

Cane Fruits: Raspberries, Loganberries and Blackberries

Time of application	Weeds controlled	Chemical name	Notes
Before weeds appear	Nearly all weeds in germinating stage	Simazine	Apply to clean moist soil, preferably in February or March.
After weeds appear	Annual weeds and shallow rooted perennials	Paraquat	Use as a directed spray on to weeds at any time of the year. Avoid wetting the foliage otherwise damage will result, though during the dormant season paraquat will not cause injury if it comes into contact with the stems.
In early spring *before* signs of bud movement	Annuals and many perennials including grass	Dichlobenil	Apply only to fruiting crops, but not after sucker emergence. Do not apply to newly planted canes within 2 years of planting.

Plums and Cherries

Time of application	Weeds controlled	Chemical name	Notes
March and repeat as frequently as necessary	Annual weeds and shallow rooted perennials	Paraquat	Apply as a directed spray, avoiding wetting the bark of trees less than 3 years old.

Strawberries

Time of application	Weeds controlled	Chemical name	Notes
December	Nearly all weeds in germinating stage	Simazine	Do not use on sandy soils. Apply to clean moist soil as an overall spray on plants which have been established for at least 4 months.
Post harvest July – August	Nearly all weeds in germinating stage	Simazine	Apply to clean moist soil following defoliation and general clean up of weeds and runners after harvest.
Any time from the end of picking to the start of flowering	Annual weeds and unwanted runners	Paraquat	Use as a very carefully directed spray avoiding the strawberry plants. Any drift onto plants will cause severe scorch and injury. Application should be by means of a dribble bar or coarse low pressure spray hooded against drift.

SOFT FRUITS

In most districts in order to obtain a crop from soft fruits, it is necessary to protect the plants from birds, both during the winter when bullfinches are the main culprits and over the ripening period when blackbirds and thrushes are troublesome. This can be done most easily by grouping all soft fruits together where a cage can be erected over them. Strawberries should not be included, as these are best grown on a 3-year rotational basis in the vegetable garden.

In its simplest form, the soft fruit cage is an enclosure of wire netting from $\frac{1}{2}$ to $\frac{3}{4}$ in. (13 to 19 mm.) mesh some 6 to 7 feet (about 2 m.) high, supported on posts. The netting at the sides remains in place all the year round. The top of the cage is covered with $\frac{3}{4}$ in. (19 mm.) mesh netting, suitably draped over battens. There are various materials available, such as terylene, plastic, polyethylene, nylon

Fruit cage of Garden No. 2 at Wisley.

and reconditioned fish netting. It is not advisable to use galvanised wire netting over the top because of the risk of damage to the plants due to zinc toxicity from condensation drips. Keep the top covered throughout the winter except when heavy falls of snow are expected. However, it is important to leave the top open during the flowering period, so

Inside the fruit cage.

that pollinating insects may enter easily. It has been found that they tend to avoid fruit bushes in a closed cage, even if the mesh of the net is comparatively large.

Another advantage of grouping soft fruits together is that their cultural requirements can be attended to without interfering with those of tree fruits. For example there may be occasions when it is necessary to spray tree fruits with fungicides and in-secticides at a time when the soft fruits are ready for harvesting.

STRAWBERRIES

The strawberry is the fruit that will give the quickest return in the shortest possible time. If the ground is well prepared, strawberries planted in late July or August will fruit in the following year. The planting of a strawberry bed is one of the first jobs to tackle in the fruit garden. Certain cultivars, for example 'Cambridge Vigour' and 'Cambridge Favourite', can however produce a useful quantity of fruit in their first year even with September planting. *It is essential that plants be obtained from a reputable source, certified as virus-tested.*

Preparation of the ground

Strawberries succeed best in soils that are rich in humus and well-drained. When digging the soil before planting (see p. 8) incorporate into it a generous dressing of well-rooted compost or farmyard manure at the rate of one barrowload to about 6 square yards (6 sq. m.) at least a month before planting. In the final cultivation just before planting work into the top few inches sulphate of potash at $\frac{1}{2}$ oz. per sq. yard (17 g/m²) and bone meal at 3 oz. per sq. yard (100 g/m²). Firm the soil, rake off any organic material left on the surface, and mark out for planting.

Planting

The rows should be not less than 30 in. (75 cm.) apart and the plants 15 to 18 in. (38 to 45 cm.) in the rows. Make a hole large enough to take the roots of the plant and

Right, top: Inserting the young strawberry plant.

Right, centre: Replacing the soil.

Right, below: Planting finished, with the crown at soil level.

plant firmly. After planting, the crown or root-stock should be level with the soil.

The best time for planting is from mid-July to mid-September, though planting may be done from July until the following April and May, provided soil and weather conditions are suitable. If a good first-year crop is required, early planting (by September) is essential.

Cultural details

After planting see that the plants are well watered. Keep down weeds by hoeing and/or herbicide application (see p. 16). Prick over the ground the following season, and as the fruits begin to weigh down the truss, lay down straw to prevent damage to the fruit by dirt in wet weather. Alternatives to loose straw are black plastic or specially made strawberry mats. It is important not to put down a thick layer of straw too early in the season since this will tend to prevent the free flow of heat upwards from the soil, so allowing frost damage on cold nights. Frost-protection during flowering can be given by spreading straw lightly over the plants on cold nights but this should be removed during the day.

After late autumn or spring planting do not allow fruiting in

the first season, but remove the blossoms to allow good strong plants to be built up for the next season. Remove runners and keep down weeds. In dry weather give plenty of water.

Protection from birds and squirrels

It will be necessary to net the whole plantation during the fruiting season. Use fish netting, plastic or nylon netting draped over battens supported on low posts, about 4 feet (1.2 m.) high. Picking is easier with nets at this height, and the birds are kept well away from the fruit.

Picking

Pick the fruits when they are fully ripe and dry. For dessert they should be picked complete with stalk. Handle the fruits with care. Strawberries for jam are picked without calyx and stalk.

After fruiting

Immediately after picking is finished cut off the old leaves using hand shears or sickle, cutting about 4 in. (10.1 cm.) above the plants so that the crowns and young leaves are not damaged. Cut off all runners, remove the old straw, foliage and weeds and burn the lot. After the plantation has been cleaned up lightly fork in sulphate of potash in between the rows at $\frac{1}{2}$ oz. per sq. yard (17 g/m²). No nitrogen fertiliser is necessary unless the soil is shallow or the plants weak. A similar manuring programme is adopted

in the third season. It seldom pays to retain strawberries for more than three years, as cropping becomes poor. Because of the spraying requirements of bush and tree fruits it is best to grow strawberries as a rotational crop in the vegetable garden. Successional beds should be maintained.

Propagation

New stock can be raised from a few healthy plants which preferably have not been allowed to fruit, but it is important to use only those which produce good trusses of flowers. The runners may be left to grow in the soil, or better, rooted into small pots in early July containing a compost of equal parts of loam, peat and sand. By early August when they are well rooted they may be severed from the parent and planted out. The importance of healthy stock must again be emphasised and the periodical renewal with Certified Stocks is most important.

Extending the season

Early strawberries can be produced by protecting the plants in the spring with continuous glass cloches or with polythene tunnels. Strawberries under cloches may be three to four weeks earlier to fruit and those under polythene

Below: Post and string supports for netting to protect the fruit from birds.

Right: A jam jar over the main support posts enables netting to be pulled easily into position, with little damage.

Strawing down is done as developing fruits weigh down the truss.

seven to fourteen days earlier than unprotected plants. At the other end of the season late strawberries can be obtained by planting perpetuals (remontants) which will crop from July until the autumn frosts though not as heavily as the summer-fruiting cultivars in their season. The summer-fruiting strawberry 'Redgauntlet' will often produce an autumn crop if it

Runners to be used for propagation are pegged down into the soil or into a pot.

has been protected in the spring. Thus by the proper use of glass or polythene and the correct choice of cultivars it is possible to pick strawberries from late May until the late autumn depending upon soil and locality.

Rooted runners severed from the parent plant. Note the amount of roots in the pot turned out.

Cultivation under cloches and polythene tunnels

In general the cultural and manurial requirements of pro-tected strawberries are the same as for strawberries in the open. Usually one-year-old plants are protected rather than two-year-olds as the latter are larger and may become too leafy or etiolated under cover. The spacing is as recommended for outdoor culture although a more economical use of the protection would be to

double up on the spacing in the row, planting at 8 to 9 in. (20 to 23 cm.) apart and then after harvesting singling the plants to 16 to 18 in. (40 to 45 cm.) apart.

TYPES OF CLOCHES

There are several types of cloche, both glass and plastic, suitable for strawberries. The most widely used is the barn cloche consisting of sides and two top pieces of glass 12 × 24 in. (30 × 60 cm.), giving a cloche 2 ft (60 cm.) long and 1 ft

(30 cm.) high and nearly 26 in. (65 cm.) wide. The sides can also be 6 or 9 in. (15 cm. or 23 cm.) high.

POLYTHENE TUNNELS

This method of protection consists of continuous tunnels made of polythene film (150 gauge) supported on galvanised wire hoops to which it is held down tightly by string ties. The usual width of polythene is 48 in. (1.2 m.). The film is stretched out tightly over the hoops and each end secured to a stout wooden peg driven into the ground. Alternatively, the ends may be buried in sufficient depth of soil to provide good anchorage.

Right: Jig for making wire hoops to support medium-size tunnels of 48-inch wide, 150g. polythene.

Below: The polythene film is stretched over the hoops and tied by twine to keep it in place. The ends are secured by tying to a post or are buried in the ground.

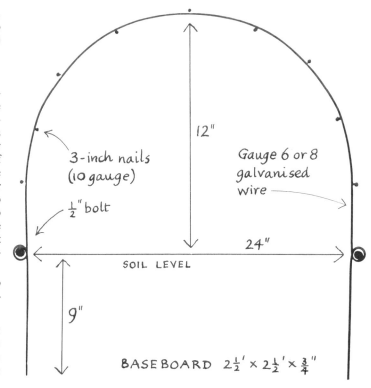

3-inch nails (10 gauge)

½" bolt

12"

Gauge 6 or 8 galvanised wire

24"

SOIL LEVEL

9"

BASEBOARD 2½' × 2½' × ¾"

The first two hoops at each end of the row are spaced 6 in. (15 cm.) apart for extra support with the remainder at 30 in. (75 cm.) apart. The hoops are made from gauge 6 or 8 galvanised wire. The rings, one on each side of the hoop, facing outwards, are formed by holding the correct length for the leg ends of the wire in a vice and pulling the wire round a small piece of tubing of $\frac{1}{2}$ in. (13 mm.) outside diameter. The wire can then be bent over an arrangement of nails in a board to produce a half circle.

USE OF CLOCHES AND POLYTHENE TUNNELS
The time to cover the plants is generally February although it can be done at any time from January to mid-March. Ventilation during the cold early days of spring will not be necessary but as the plants start flowering some ventilation must be given particularly on warm sunny days to help pollination and to prevent the build up of too high temperatures which can result in weak drawn growth and fruit malformation. The cloches are moved wider apart to allow more air movement and the sides of the polythene tunnels are pushed up on one side.

Ventilation should be continued throughout as it has been found that, if the cloches or tunnels are kept closed, early strawberries may be achieved but at the expense of size of fruit, weight of crop and flavour.

CHOICE OF CULTIVARS
Any of the ordinary summer fruiting cultivars can be used. The heaviest cropping though not the best flavoured are 'Cambridge Favourite' and 'Redgauntlet'. The early cultivars 'Cambridge Prizewinner' and 'Cambridge Vigour' are of good flavour, and 'Royal Sovereign' though poor in yield is considered to be the best in quality. 'Redgauntlet' has the additional advantage in that if protected in the spring under glass or polythene it will yield a second crop in the autumn following a warm summer.

Immediately after the protected crop has been cleared the glass or polythene should be removed and the old foliage cut off. Also remove any runners. A light dressing of sulphate of ammonia should then be applied keeping the fertiliser clear of the crowns.

Perpetual (remontant) strawberries
Perpetual strawberries will carry on the succession of fruit after summer-fruiting cultivars are over. The amount picked at any one time is not great, but plants will fruit more or less continuously from July to the end of November when poor light and frosts finally stop development.

Cultural requirements are similar to those of the ordinary strawberry, but perpetuals are gross feeders and intolerant of drought. Early flowers can be removed to ensure good pickings from August onwards.

No certification scheme has yet been organised for these plants: it is as well therefore to assume that they are carrying virus and to plant them as far as possible from summer-fruiting certified plants.

The soil should be very fertile and high in organic material to improve its moisture holding capacity. During dry weather water copiously. Plant from August to October, or in the spring. Late autumn planting is inadvisable as the young plants may not become sufficiently established to withstand the winter.

Recommended cultivars
EARLY
Pantagruella
Cambridge Prizewinner
Gorella
Cambridge Rival*
Grandee
Cambridge Vigour* (one-year plants)
Royal Sovereign*

* Specially recommended for flavour and quality.

MID-SEASON TO LATE
Tamella
Cambridge Favourite
Redgauntlet
Cambridge Vigour (two-year plants and older)
Talisman*
Montrose
Merton Dawn
Cambridge Late Pine*
PERPETUAL OR REMONTANT
Gento
Rabunda
St Claude
PROMISING NEW CULTIVARS
Tenira, *mid-season*
Aromel, *perpetual*

Pests
APHIDS (greenflies) breed rapidly on new growths from May onwards and, in addition to weakening and fouling infested plants, may spread virus diseases. Spray with malathion or nicotine in early May and at other times if colonies are seen on the plants.

SLUGS eat ripening strawberries and are best controlled by baiting with slug pellets well before the crop starts to fruit. High humidity and the use of organic fertilisers and mulches tend to encourage slugs.

GLASSHOUSE RED SPIDER MITES infest the leaves of strawberry plants and can cause severe discoloration, bronzing and death, especially on plants grown in cloches or polythene tunnels. Thorough spraying with malathion may give some control but too frequent use will result in the pest developing resistance. Biological control with the predatory mite (*Phytoseiulus*), is possible if stocks can be obtained but is unlikely to work well if non-selective insecticides are used against aphids as these will kill off the predators.

EELWORMS, TARSONEMID MITES AND VIRUS DISEASES all produce superficially similar symptoms of stunting, distortion and discoloration. Expert diagnosis and advice on treatment should be sought if such symptoms appear in a crop, or, failing this, severely affected plants

Left, a virus-infected strawberry plant. Right, a healthy plant.

should be dug up and burned immediately.

Diseases

VIRUS DISEASES are very troublesome on strawberries causing stunting and a poor or no crop. Affected plants show leaf symptoms, such as yellow edges, yellow or purplish mottling or blotching, or crinkling. These should be dug up and burned as they cannot be cured. New stock certified as free of virus disease should be obtained and planted on a fresh site, or in new soil, as some viruses are transmitted by eelworms in the soil. The commonest virus diseases of strawberries are spread by aphids (see above).

GREY MOULD caused by the fungus *Botrytis cinerea* can result in serious losses of fruit in a wet summer. Affected berries rot and become covered with a brownish grey fluffy growth. As soon as the first flowers open, spray with dichlofluanid (not to be used on strawberries under glass or polythene) and repeat three times at 10-day intervals; *or* spray with benomyl repeating twice at 10- to 14-day intervals; *or* spray with thiophanate-methyl repeating twice at 14-day intervals. Thiram and captan can also be used except on fruit for canning, bottling and deep freezing. Pick off affected fruits and remove them from the strawberry plot.

STRAWBERRY MILDEW affects the fruit, causing it to lose its shine; the leaves turn purple and curl upwards showing greyish lower surfaces. Spray immediately pre-blossom with $1\frac{1}{2}\%$ lime sulphur *or* dinocap, repeating at 10- to 14-day intervals until 1 or 2 weeks before harvest; *or* spray with benomyl *or* thiophanate-methyl at early flower stage repeating twice at 14-day intervals; *or* dust with sulphur. To avoid possible taint, lime sulphur and sulphur should not be used on ripening fruit to be canned or frozen.

After harvesting, remove leaves by cutting or burning off, or spray again with one of the above fungicides.

LEAF SPOTS can be produced by several different fungi and show as circular purple, red or white spots, particularly on old leaves. In severe cases withering and disintegration of the leaves occurs.

LEAF BLOTCH produces larger brown blotches with a purple border; blackening and rotting of the leaf and flower stalks occurs followed by withering of fruits and death of leaves. Remove and burn any withered leaves and those showing severe spotting. If the trouble persists and much withering of fruit and leaves occurs, spray the following spring just after growth starts using a 0.2% solution of zineb, and repeat a fortnight later *or* spray with dichlofluanid 2 to 3 weeks before flowering and again 10 to 14 days later.

RASPBERRIES

The raspberry is another fruit for quick cropping and comparatively heavy yields. A yield of a pound (0.45 kg.) per foot (30 cm.) of row per season is not uncommon.

It is most important to start with healthy plants, if possible canes certified under the Ministry of Agriculture certification scheme. Starting with healthy plants a row of raspberries should last at least eight years before starting to degenerate with virus infection. Then choose a new site for replanting. If this is not possible the old area should be re-soiled. Raspberries prefer a slightly acid soil. Soils with a high lime content can cause chlorotic foliage (see p. 10).

If there is a choice of position raspberries should be given a situation sheltered from strong winds. They will grow satisfactorily in partial shade.

Preparation of site and ground

Prepare the ground early in the autumn. Raspberries require a good supply of organic matter in the soil, and have a high potash requirement. Although they have masses of fibrous surface roots, they are also deep-rooting; for this reason apply manure mixed with the soil at the bottom of the trench. In a light soil dig in as much farmyard manure or rotted compost as can be obtained. Raspberries in poor soils fail to grow satisfactorily and the fruits

lack flavour.

Planting

The best time to plant is in November, but it can be done at any time in the winter, up to April. Plant the young cane so that the root is covered by about 3 in. (7.5 cm.) of soil and make the ground firm. The canes are spaced at about 18 in. (45 cm.) apart with about six feet (1.8 m.) between the rows. It is an advantage to plant in rows running north and south which allows evenness in growth.

The canes should be cut down to 9 to 12 in. (23 to 30 cm.) above the ground soon after planting. Then the plants will become well established in the first summer with good growth and canes. Plants allowed to fruit in their first season will not become well established. By the second year after planting, the young canes, which have grown up during the first summer, should be full of

Planting out the new canes.

vigour and capable of bearing a useful crop of fruit.

Cultivation and manuring

Keep weeds down by hoeing or the use of herbicides (see p. 16).

In established rows do not cultivate the ground close up to the canes. The surface roots will not then be disturbed and the new canes will have every opportunity of growing and ripening. Remove thin weakly canes. Lawn mowings, rotted manure or composted material used as a mulch early in May every year will help to keep the soil moist and feed the canes. This mulch, together with an annual application in March of sulphate of potash at the rate of $\frac{3}{4}$ oz. to the square yard (25 g. to the sq.m.) will provide adequate nutrients.

Training

To obtain clean good quality fruit it is necessary to tie the fruiting canes onto a permanent wire fence system. The usual method is to have two or three wires strained horizontally and stapled to wooden posts at 2 ft (60 cm.), $3\frac{1}{2}$ ft (1 m.) and 5 ft (1.5 m.) from the ground, although for vigorous cultivars, e.g. 'Norfolk Giant', it is advisable to have the top wire at about 6 ft (1.8 m.). The end posts must be strutted.

Another simple method is to use two parallel wires at about 4 ft (1.2 m.) separated horizontally by short pieces of wood, and grow the canes between the wires without tying them in. However, the canes are liable to wind damage because they are not tied individually. Temporary support can be given with stout string made secure with cross ties.

Picking

For home use (dessert, freezing or jamming) the fruits are picked

Left, above: Cutting back newly-planted canes.

Left: Pulling up unwanted suckers close to the row. Those between the rows are hoed out.

Above: Raspberry canes tied in to wires supported by wooden posts.

Left: After cutting out the old canes and tying in the new.

Right: Shortening the tips in spring.

without the stalk and core. Fruits for showing are picked with the stalk attached, using scissors.

Pruning

As soon as fruiting is over cut off the old canes as close to the ground as possible to make room for the new young canes which are to bear the next crop. Select the strongest and healthiest of the new canes, retaining not more than eight per plant, tying them securely to the wires and spacing the canes 3 to 4 in. (7.5 to 10 cm.) apart along the top wire. Towards the end of the winter or in early spring the canes retained are shortened to 6 in. (15 cm.) above the top wire. Do not leave too much cane without support as the top is liable to snap under the weight of fruit. An alternative to tipping is to bend the top of the canes over and tie them again to the top wire. Cutting off too much of the tips will reduce yields.

Propagation

Raspberries are easily propagated from suckers forked up from the ground in or near the rows. But the plants must be healthy. Virus-infected canes are worse than useless as not only will the yield from them be low but they are a source of infection for other canes. They should be dug up and burnt.

Autumn-fruiting raspberries

Most raspberries bear fruit on canes which were produced the previous year, but there are some which carry their fruit on canes of the current year's growth. They do not yield as heavily as summer fruiting raspberries but will give a worthwhile crop from September to November. In established rows cut all canes down at the end of February to within a few inches of the ground. Fruits will then be borne in the autumn at the tips of the new canes produced since pruning. Newly planted canes are treated as shown on page 26.

Recommended cultivars

SUMMER-FRUITING
Malling Promise, *early-mid-season*
Glen Clova★, *early-mid-season*
Lloyd George, *early-mid-season, very good flavour*
Malling Delight, *mid-season, good flavour*
Malling Jewel★, *mid-season, good flavour*
Malling Orion, *mid-season*
Malling Admiral★, *late, good flavour*
Norfolk Giant, *late, good for preserving*
Leo★, *late, good for preserving*

AUTUMN-FRUITING
September
Zeva
Heritage

★ Good for freezing.

Left, above: Lifting suckers in winter for replanting.

Left, below: Old fruiting canes of a summer-fruiting raspberry are cut out after fruiting or in the autumn. Above: All canes of established autumn-fruiting raspberries are cut down to ground level at the end of February.

PROMISING NEW CULTIVARS

Malling Delight, *early-mid-season*
Glen Isla, *late season*

Pests

RASPBERRY BEETLES lay eggs in the blossom and the grubs feed on the ripening fruit. They are often first noticed when the fruit is picked. Spray or dust the young fruitlets with malathion or derris when the first pink fruit is seen.

APHIDS are potentially serious pests as they spread virus diseases but the prevention of virus transmission is not easy. 5% tar-oil applied thoroughly to the dormant canes in December or January will kill off overwintering eggs, and spraying malathion, dimethoate or formothion just before the blossom opens will kill any aphids that have escaped the winter treatment.

Diseases

VIRUS DISEASES, which may be aphid- or eelworm-borne, frequently cause yellow mottling or blotching of the leaves, which may be distorted, and canes will eventually lose vigour and cropping capacity. Affected canes and stools should be removed and burnt, as they cannot be cured. The soil should be changed or another site chosen for new disease-free canes.

SPUR BLIGHT shows around the nodes on the canes as blotches which are first purple and then silver. Buds at affected nodes die and any shoots produced die back in spring. Burn badly diseased canes. Spray with bordeaux mixture or liquid copper when buds are ½ in. (13 mm.) long and again when the tips of the flowers are just showing white. Better control, however, can be achieved by spraying with benomyl, dichlofluanid, thiram or captan, starting soon after new canes emerge and repeating three or four times at fortnightly intervals. Thiophanate-methyl can also be used, the first application being given when the buds have grown out ½ inch (13 mm.) and repeating at 14-day intervals to the end of flowering.

CANE SPOT affects canes, leaves and fruit, showing first as small purple spots and then as elliptical greyish blotches with a purple margin. Remove and burn badly diseased canes. Spray with 5% lime sulphur at bud burst and 2½% lime sulphur immediately before flower, *or* use liquid copper at these times, *or* thiram except on fruit to be processed. Benomyl or thiophanate-methyl can also be used, the first application given when the buds are ½ in. (13 mm.) long and repeated at 14-day intervals to the end of flowering.

CANE BLIGHT causes withering of leaves and dieback of fruiting canes due to infection at ground level where a dark area develops on the canes; affected canes become brittle and snap off easily. Cut diseased canes hard back to below soil level and burn them, and disinfect the pruning tool. As the new canes grow, spray with bordeaux mixture or other copper fungicide.

HONEY FUNGUS often causes the rapid death of canes (see p. 77).

GREY MOULD is sometimes troublesome on the fruit. For control, spray with dichlofluanid, benomyl or thiophanate methyl (for details see strawberry, p. 24).

IRON DEFICIENCY (see p. 10) shows as irregular yellowing between the veins. It is frequent on raspberries and should not be confused with symptoms due to viruses.

BLACK CURRANTS

Black currants prefer an open sunny position, but will tolerate partial shade. If suitable cultivars are planted for a succession, they can provide fresh fruit from the end of June until early August. The fruit is high in vitamin C content; it is excellent for jam. Very heavy yields can be obtained from established bushes. Moreover potentially they have a very long life.

Black currants produce the best fruit on one-year-old wood, i.e. on growth made in the preceding year. Cultivation, therefore, is aimed at encouraging as much new growth as possible.

When planning a new plantation, be careful to procure young bushes from a reputable source. It is best to buy two-year-old

Below, left: A well-rooted, two-year-old black currant bush ready for planting.

Below, right: A young bush in position awaiting return of soil.

Certified bushes. One-year-old plants do not carry a certificate though they are quite acceptable provided they have been propagated from healthy stock.

Preparation of ground
Black currants are tolerant of a wide range of soils provided they are retentive of moisture and are well drained. They require quantities of manure or compost in order to grow them satisfactorily especially on light soils. Black

Left: Black currants are planted deeper than in the nursery to encourage shoot production from the base.

Above: Newly planted bush cut hard back.

Left, below: Cutting out some of the old wood from the base.

currants respond particularly to generous manuring.

Planting

This may be done at any time between October and March but the earlier the better. Allow plenty of room between the bushes. Do not plant less than 5 feet (1.5 m.) apart with 6 feet (1.8 m.) between the rows, as in a few years' time the bushes will have become large and spreading. It is essential to allow light and air to the bushes. Plant firmly and deeply, so that strong new growths are readily produced from the base.

Pruning

After planting cut back all the shoots to within an inch (2.5 cm.) of soil level. The bushes should not be allowed to fruit in the first season after planting. The energies of the bush should be directed to building up the growth of the new shoots which will be produced after cutting back. It is on the strongest of these shoots that fruit will be borne in the second summer from planting.

In the first autumn after planting cut down the weakest of the new shoots to soil level; further shoots will then be produced in

the following year and these will later bear fruit. As the bush gets older and becomes established, annual pruning consists of cutting out between $\frac{1}{4}$ and $\frac{1}{3}$ of the old wood, so letting in light and air to help in ripening the new wood on which is to be borne most of the following year's crop. The best time to prune is after the fruit has been picked, but it can also be done in the autumn. Old neglected bushes, provided they are healthy, may be rejuvenated by cutting them down to within a few inches of the ground and allowing the strongest and best-placed new shoots to grow on for a season to produce fruit the next year.

Cultivation

Black currants thrive on heavy manuring. Well-rotted farmyard manure is the best material, but decomposed lawn-mowings mixed with old poultry manure or other composts make good substitutes. They may be applied whenever available. Nitro-chalk (or on alkaline soils, sulphate of ammonia) applied in March at the rate of about 1 oz. to the square yard (33 g/m^2) will promote growth. On light soils a straw mulch is of great advantage in conserving moisture and keeping down weeds but beware of fire.

Do not dig near the bushes. Weeds should be kept down by hoeing or by herbicides. On most soils bushes will benefit by thorough watering during dry periods.

Picking

If the fruit is to be used within a short time it may be stripped from the stalk or strig when picking, but it will keep in better condition and be more easily handled afterwards if the strig is pulled off with fruit attached.

Propagation

Cuttings about 8 inches (20 cm.)

Left, above: Established bush before pruning.

Left: The same bush after pruning.

Right: Current year's growths suitable for cuttings.

Far right: Cuttings prepared for insertion; no buds are removed.

long are taken during the autumn from healthy young shoots of current year's growth and the unripened top removed. Cut off the base close to a bud. Do not remove any of the basal buds as these will grow out at or below ground level making the 'stool'. Make a series of clefts with a spade in the ground, which, in heavy soil, should be given a sprinkling of sand in the bottom. Insert the cuttings some six inches (15 cm.) apart to a depth of 5 or 6 inches (12 to 15 cm.) leaving two buds above ground level, and make quite firm by treading. By the following autumn the cuttings will have rooted and are then transferred to their permanent quarters.

Recommended cultivars
Boskoop Giant, *early*
Laxton's Giant, *early*
Mendip Cross, *early*
Tor Cross, *early*
Seabrook's Black, *second early*
Blackdown, *second early; resistant to mildew*
Blacksmith, *mid-season*
Raven, *mid-season*
Wellington XXX, *mid-season*
Cotswold Cross, *mid-season*
Baldwin, *late*
Westwick Choice, *late*
Malvern Cross, *late*
Amos Black, *very late, light cropper*
Jet, *very late*

Promising new cultivars
Ben Lomond, *mid-season to late*
Ben Nevis, *mid-season to late*

Freezing
Most cultivars freeze well. High in vitamin C are Baldwin, Boskoop Giant and Westwick Choice, Also good are Cotswold Cross, Mendip Cross, Seabrook's Black,

Cuttings inserted in a shallow trench to leave about 2 buds above soil level.

Wellington XXX and Malvern Cross.

Pests

BLACK CURRANT GALL MITE is the most important pest as it destroys buds and also transmits reversion disease. The minute mites feed and breed within the buds throughout the year and migrate to young buds in the spring. Hand-picking and burning the 'big buds' may limit infestations and spraying ½ to 1% lime sulphur when the first flowers open and again after three weeks will also give some control.

APHIDS infest leaves and stems. Control by spraying with 5% tar-oil winter wash during the dormant period or with malathion, dimethoate or formothion applied just before flowering.

Diseases

REVERSION is a serious disease which causes a severe reduction in crop. Although certain typical symptoms are produced on flower buds and leaves, these are difficult for an amateur to identify and specialist advice is best sought in June or July, if bushes fail to give a satisfactory crop. Once confirmed, diseased bushes should be dug up and burned.

LEAF SPOT produces small dark brown spots which coalesce until the whole leaf surface becomes brown. Affected leaves fall prematurely and there may be a reduction in crop the following season. Spray immediately after flowering

Big bud mite-infected shoot on the left. Healthy shoot on the right.

with zineb, repeat at 10 to 14-day intervals to within a month of picking and repeat after harvesting, or spray then with a copper fungicide.

Thiophanate-methyl will also control this disease if applied just as the first flowers open, repeating two or three times at fortnightly intervals. Benomyl can be applied at the grape stage (before the flowers open) repeating three times at 14-day intervals and post harvest every 14 days if necessary. Rake up and burn diseased leaves.

AMERICAN GOOSEBERRY MILDEW is sometimes troublesome late in the season (see under gooseberry, p. 41).

HONEY FUNGUS can cause the rapid death of bushes (see p. 77).

RED AND WHITE CURRANTS

The method of growth and consequently the pruning of red and white currants is quite different from that of black currants. The white currant is a variety of the red and requires similar treatment. Red currants fruit on short spurs made on the old wood and in clusters at the base of young growths made the previous year; some fruit is also borne on these young shoots. Red currants are capable of producing a large quantity of fruit in a small space and can be grown either as bushes or cordons. The latter are particularly suitable for small gardens, and can be trained on walls or fences. Single-stemmed, double or triple cordons can be grown.

Red and white currants benefit from the incorporation of composted material or farmyard manure into the ground before planting but do not have the same high demand for nitrogen as black currants. They are, however, very susceptible to potash deficiency.

Planting
There is no certification scheme for red currants, nevertheless it is important to obtain the bushes from a reliable source. Any time between October and March is suitable for planting, but the earlier the better. Two-year-old bushes are spaced at 5 ft (1.5 m.) apart with 6 ft (1.8 m.) between

the rows. Single cordons may be planted 15 in. (38 cm.) apart allowing more room for double and triple cordons. Plant firmly. Cordons should be staked.

Cultivation
Mulching with rotted farmyard manure, especially when the bushes are young, is beneficial. Sulphate of potash, at the rate of about $\frac{3}{4}$ oz. to the square yard (25 g. to the sq. m.), or liberal dressings of bonfire ash, should be given in early spring. Any suckers arising from the leg or from below ground are removed. A short leg to the bush of 9 in. to 1 ft (23 to 30 cm.) is useful in keeping the fruit above the level of dirt splashes. Strong young shoots are sometimes apt to be broken out in gusty summer winds; while a bush is young it is worth while staking and tying those shoots which are of importance to the growth and shape of the plant.

Right: A U-cordon of red currant.

Far right: Two-year-old red currant; note the 'leg'.

35

Above: Planting the red currant; the roots are well spread out.

Above, centre: After planting the branches are cut back by about half.

Above right: A. A three-year-old bush before winter pruning. B. The same bush after removing or cutting back side shoots. C. The same bush after cutting back the leaders.

Pruning

WINTER. On a two-year-old bush cut each branch back by half to an outside bud. New branches will then be formed. Subsequent winter pruning will depend on the growth made; shorten the leading shoots by about half and cut back the laterals to within two buds of their base. After a few years it will be necessary to cut the year's growth back to an inch (2.5 cm.) or even less. Old branches should be cut out and new growths allowed to replace them. With cordons, cut back the laterals to about half an inch and shorten the leader by one third.

SUMMER. At the end of June shorten the laterals to some five leaves; do not shorten the leaders. With cordons shorten the laterals to five leaves but do not cut the leader until the desired maximum height is reached.

Propagation

New plants are easily grown from cuttings in the same way as for black currants (see p. 32). With currants cuttings should be 12 in. (30 cm.) long or more. Before

insertion remove all buds except the top 3 or 4, so allowing the formation of the 'leg'. After the cuttings have rooted they are planted out and then trained in the form required. A bush is formed by cutting back the young shoots in winter to about four buds. Thereafter prune as advised above.

For cordons the leading or topmost shoot is allowed to form the main stem, cutting back the sideshoots below; or a new main stem

Above: Established bush before pruning.

may be produced by cutting down a one-year-old plant to the ground and concentrating growth on a strong new stem, which will grow as a result of the cutting back; pinch back others. For a double cordon two main stems are selected and for a triple, three stems. Cordons need to be firmly staked during training.

B

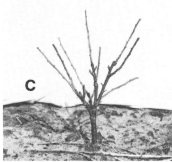

C

Above: The same bush after pruning.

Recommended cultivars

RED

Jonkheer van Tets★, *very early*
Earliest of Fourlands, *early*
Laxton's No. 1★, *early*
Red Lake★, *mid-season*
Rondom, *late*
Wilson's Long Bunch, *late*

★ Good flavour.

WHITE

White Grape★, *mid-season*
White Dutch, *mid-season*
White Leviathan, *mid-season*
White Versailles, *mid-season*

Pests

BIRDS, especially pigeons and blackbirds, attack ripe fruits, and in many areas damage can only be

Right, above: Branch of an established bush before pruning.
Right: After pruning.

37

Far left: Current year's growths suitable for cuttings.

Left: Cuttings prepared for insertion. The lower buds have been removed.

Left, below: Cuttings inserted in the shallow trench. Note the length of cutting left above the soil.

avoided by erecting netting to exclude them.

APHIDS infest leaves and shoots but can be controlled by a 5% tar-oil spray applied to dormant bushes during the winter, or by malathion, dimethoate or formothion sprays applied just before blossoming.

Diseases

CORAL SPOT shows as numerous coral-red spots on old and dead wood and can cause die back of branches or even death of a plant. Cut out and burn the affected branches to a point well below diseased tissues and paint all the wounds with a good protective paint.

LEAF SPOT causes small brown spots on the leaves which eventually wither and fall prematurely. Spray as for black currants (see p. 34).

GOOSEBERRIES

Gooseberries are easily grown and are tolerant of a wide range of conditions. For the area of ground covered they give a large quantity of fruit. The gooseberry is usually grown as a bush on a short leg, but it can also be grown in trained forms such as single, double or even triple cordons, or fan-shaped specimens can be trained against walls and fences. The fruit is borne on one-year-old shoots and spurs on the older shoots or, in the case of a cordon, on the main stem.

Preparation of ground

A well drained, moist loamy soil suits gooseberries best. It is particularly important that the ground is free of perennial weeds such as couch grass and bindweed. If the soil is light, the addition of liberal quantities of farmyard manure or compost before planting will be beneficial and without this preparation dessert cultivars such as 'Leveller' will not do well. Heavy soils which tend to pack down hard will be made more friable by the generous addition of bulky organic manures. Sulphate of potash at the rate of $\frac{3}{4}$ oz. to the square yard (25 g. to the sq. m.) should be lightly forked into the soil during the final preparation.

Planting

Plant any time during autumn and winter when conditions are suitable. If possible, two- or three-year-old bushes should be planted about 5 to 6 feet (1.5 to 1.8 m.) apart. For single cordons 1 foot (30 cm.) apart will be sufficient. Allow plenty of room for the roots and plant firmly but not too deeply. Trained specimens will require staking as soon as the soil has settled down.

Pruning

WINTER. The shoots of a two- or three-year-old bush should be cut back about half-way to an appropriate bud – according to whether the cultivar is of drooping or upright growth; if it is a 'drooper' cut back to an upward-pointing bud. Subsequently for a few years cut the new leading growths back about half way. This should produce strong branches for the support of heavy crops of fruit. The formation of fruiting spurs will be encouraged by cutting back lateral growths to about 3 in. (7.5 cm.). Remove all weak growths.

After some years the leading shoots of an established bush may be cut harder. Cut out weak growths and old wood and thin any main branches if the centre is too thick. Vigorous young growths will eventually take the place of old main branches that are removed. Cut out crossing branches.

With cordons and trained forms shorten the side-shoots to three buds; fruit spurs will then be formed. When the leading shoots of cordons become inconveniently long they may be cut back each year.

SUMMER. From the third week in June shorten all the lateral shoots to about five leaves. This applies to all types of training, including cordons. By summer pruning in this way the formation of fruit buds is encouraged. Moreover, any tips infected with American gooseberry mildew are removed.

Left: Established gooseberry bush before winter pruning.

Right: The same bush after pruning.

Above: Branch of an established bush before winter pruning.

Above, right: The same branch after pruning.

Cultivation

Digging the ground between gooseberry bushes should be avoided as deep digging will cause root damage. Weeds should be rigorously kept down by shallow hoeing or by application of herbicides. Should any basal growths appear from the ground tear them out, otherwise the advantage of growing the bush on a leg will be lost and the bush will grow out of shape.

If the bushes are not grown in a cage, protection of the fruit buds from birds may be necessary during the late winter, done by winding black cotton amongst the branches. If bushes have been attacked it is best to delay winter pruning until the buds are just beginning to break so that cuts can be made to a living bud.

Careful manuring is an important factor in growing good fruit. The ground should be mulched with well-rotted farmyard manure or composted material during the winter. Ample supplies of potash are necessary as gooseberries are very susceptible to a deficiency. Sulphate of potash applied in the early spring every year at the rate of about $\frac{3}{4}$ oz. to the square yard (22 g. to the sq. m.) will suit their requirements. Ashes from the garden bonfire are also useful. If the edges of leaves look scorched it is usually a sign of potash deficiency; apply a dressing of sulphate of potash without delay.

Picking

If the bushes are carrying heavy crops the fruits can be thinned when they are half grown. The thinnings are useful for cooking, and the remaining fruits will be larger.

Propagation

Young bushes can be grown from cuttings in the same way as described for red currants (p. 36) but they do not root so readily. It is usual to remove the lower buds leaving about four at the top on well-ripened wood from which the young branches will develop. But it has been found that gooseberries root better if all the buds are left on the cutting. One year later the rooted cuttings are dug up when dormant, and the lower side shoots removed, thus creating the necessary leg, before replanting. Cuttings are taken in mid to late September.

Recommended cultivars

GREEN

Keepsake (Berry's Early Kent), *late, but the earliest for picking for tarts etc.*

Green Gem*, *mid-season*

Careless, *mid-season*

Howard's Lancer, *mid-season-late*

RED

May Duke, *early*

Whinham's Industry, *mid-season*

Lancashire Lad, *late, resistance to mildew*

Lord Derby★, *mid-season*
WHITE
Whitesmith, *mid-season*
White Lion, *late*
YELLOW
Leveller★, *mid-season*
Golden Drop, *mid-season*
FREEZING
'Careless', 'Keepsake' and immature 'Leveller' are recommended.

Pests

BULLFINCHES eat the buds in winter and there may be hardly any left after severe attacks. 'Leveller' is particularly susceptible. Erecting netting over the plants from about November to April is the only certain preventive measure.

GOOSEBERRY SAWFLY and MAGPIE MOTH caterpillars feed extensively on the leaves, reducing infested leaves to a skeleton of veins. Look out for the first signs of attack from May onwards. Hand-pick and destroy caterpillars, if possible, otherwise spray or dust with malathion or derris after flowering is over.

Diseases

AMERICAN GOOSEBERRY MILDEW affects leaves, shoots and fruits, producing a white powdery coating. Diseased shoots become distorted at the tips and should be cut out.

Spray with $1\frac{1}{2}\%$ lime sulphur (except ripening fruits to be processed and sulphur-shy cultivars, i.e. 'Careless', 'Early Sulphur', 'Leveller', 'Lord Derby', 'Roaring Lion' and 'Golden Drop') just before the flowers open; repeat after the fruit has set and again 3 weeks later: *or* use dinocap or washing soda ($\frac{1}{2}$ lb. (0.22 kg.) to

Above, left: Current year's growths suitable for cuttings.

Above, right: Cuttings prepared; note all the lower buds removed.

Right: Cuttings inserted; note the depth of insertion.

★ Recommended for flavour.

Gooseberry mildew on fruits and shoots.

$2\frac{1}{2}$ gall. (11 l.) of water, plus spreader), starting at pre-blossom and repeating as necessary but stop spraying 1–2 weeks before harvesting: *or* apply benomyl *or* thiophanate-methyl as the first flowers open and repeat two or three times at 14-day intervals. If necessary, spray again after har-·vesting with any of these fungicides.

LEAF SPOT commonly causes spotting and premature leaf fall. Spray immediately after flowering with zineb, repeat at 10- to 14-day intervals to within a month of picking and repeat after harvesting, or spray them with a copper fungicide.

GREY MOULD. Die back of a bush branch by branch until the whole plant is killed may be due to grey mould. Cut out all dead wood back into living tissues, paint the larger wounds, prune to provide plenty of light and air within a bush and see that soil conditions are good.

HONEY FUNGUS can cause a rapid death of bushes (see p. 77).

BLACKBERRIES AND HYBRID BERRIES

There are several species and cultivars of blackberries as well as some related hybrid berries suitable for garden cultivation. Some are much less rampant in growth than others and thus more suitable for growing in small areas. The loganberry, in particular, is easily controlled and is valuable for the small fruit garden. Training and some pruning are necessary for the best fruit.

They can be grown in rows or trained against walls and over arches, and are excellent for training against boundary fences. Blackberries and loganberries will succeed in both heavy and light soils and in a semi-shady position. Cultivation is simple and they are not demanding, but the most satisfactory results are achieved in a fairly heavy loam with a deep, moist root-run and where they can be grown in full sun. Deep digging before planting is essential and if the soil is light the addition of old manure when digging is desirable.

Planting

Plant between October and March whenever the weather is suitable. Young canes or rooted tips should be planted not less than 6 feet (1.8 m.) and preferably 10 feet (3 m.) apart, but some strong-

Right, above: Planting a young blackberry; the roots are well spread out.

Right: After planting. The new shoot is pointed out. The old stem is cut back to 9 inches.

Left: A plant in winter with the young wood tied along the top wire. The old wood has already been cut out.

Left, below: In early spring the one-year-old canes are separated out and tied to the wires.

growing blackberries may need even more room. Allow 6 or 7 feet (about 2 m.) between rows.

Pruning and training
After planting, cut down the young plant to within 9 inches (23 cm.) of the ground and apply a mulch of old manure if available.

As new growths arise tie them back to stakes or to wires strained on posts in the rows. A system of three or four wires one foot (30 cm.) apart, the top one about 5½ feet (1.5 m.) high, is a suitable arrangement.

After the first year a method of training should be adopted so that the current year's growths can be tied in and kept separate from the older canes bearing the fruit.

Cut out the old canes that have fruited as soon as possible. Re-tie the young canes so that the maximum amount of light and air reaches them.

Cultivation
Keeping weeds down and giving a mulch of old manure or compost will be all that is necessary. When no organic manure is available, a nitrogenous fertiliser such as sulphate of ammonia at 2 oz. to the square yard (66 g. to the sq. m.) should be applied in spring.

Propagation
Tips of shoots bent down and layered by a wire or the weight of a stone at the end of July, root readily; a hole about 6 in. (15 cm.) deep is made and the tip 'planted' firmly therein. The rooted tips or young plants can be severed from

Right, top: A loganberry in summer. The young wood has been trained up the middle of the fan.

Right: Different methods of training blackberries, loganberries etc.

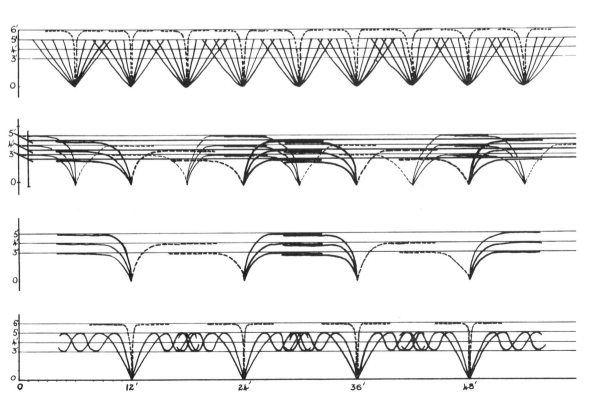

the parent plant and will be ready for removal in the spring.

Recommended cultivars
All freeze satisfactorily.

BLACKBERRIES

Bedford Giant. *Medium vigour. Fruit large to very large, very sweet but no pronounced black-berry flavour. Early (July).*

Himalaya Giant (Theodor Reimers). *Very vigorous, and thorny. Moderate flavour. Early to mid-season.*

Merton Early. *Early to mid-season. Moderate growth.*

Parsley-leaved or Cutleaf. *Vigorous. Good blackberry flavour. Ornamental foliage. Mid-season to late.*

Oregon Thornless. *A thornless form of the parsley-leaved black-berry.*

John Innes. *Vigorous. Good sweet flavour. Excellent cropper. Late.*

HYBRID BERRIES

Loganberry. *Medium vigour. Good flavour. A number of poor cropping stocks are in existence but a healthy heavy cropping clonal stock is available LY59).*

Thornless Loganberry. *A thornless sport of the loganberry. A healthy stock which crops as well as the thorned is now available. (L654).*

Boysenberry. *Large black-red fruits. Canes up to eight feet long. There is a thornless form.*

Japanese Wineberry, *Rubus phoenicolasius. Both canes and fruit are decorative. More of an ornamental than a fruit crop.*

Kings Acre Berry. *Dark shiny red fruits, medium size.*

Tayberry. *Large fruits, mild sweet flavour, early.*

Pests
RASPBERRY BEETLE grubs attack the fruits of loganberries and blackberries, and can be controlled by spraying or dusting with malathion or derris, applied as soon as most of the blossom falls, with a repeat application when the first fruit is colouring.

Diseases
CANE SPOT (see p. 29) can be troublesome on loganberry and other hybrid berries. Remove and burn diseased canes. Spray with bordeaux mixture or liquid copper immediately before flowering and again as soon as the fruit has set, or use thiram at these times except on fruit to be processed. Benomyl and thiophanate-methyl could probably also be used to control cane spot on these cane fruits.

SPUR BLIGHT (see p. 29) can affect loganberries.

VIRUS DISEASES can cause stunting of canes and a reduction in crop. Diseased plants should be burned and healthy plants obtained.

TREE OR TOP FRUITS

General

The form of fruit trees, particularly those planted in the private garden, has changed considerably during this century. This is largely due to the standardisation of dwarfing rootstocks developed after research at East Malling Research Station.

In the small gardens which are usual today, there is no room for one large spreading tree. Planting several small trees whose growth can be restricted by pruning enables a wide range of different fruits to be grown in a limited space. When space is limited cultivars of high quality, particularly for eating, which are difficult to obtain in the shops, will be the choice. It is nearly always easier and cheaper to buy cooking apples than good dessert ones. With careful selection of cultivars according to the recommended lists (see individual fruits) it is possible to have apples and pears maturing in good condition from August till the following April or May. When choosing, one should remember that early dessert apples and pears last in good condition for only a short time, so it is unwise to grow too many. Late apples, and to a certain extent pears, can be kept in good condition over a long period.

A dwarf bush apple grown on a dwarfing stock is the most easily managed form of tree.

Site and aspect

Top fruits are successfully grown over a wide range of districts in Britain at altitudes between sea level and 400 feet (122 m.) or even more. South slopes warm up early, causing early flowering. They are usually drier and get more sunlight than northern slopes and the fruit is generally of good quality; but the early blossom runs a greater risk of damage by spring frosts. A site where cold spring air can drain away to lower ground is preferable to one in a frost pocket. If, however, the garden is situated in an area liable to spring frosts, the effect of frost can be reduced by planting late-flowering cultivars e.g. 'Crawley Beauty' or those with some degree of resistance to frost (such as 'Epicure', 'James Grieve', 'Ellison's Orange', 'Superb', 'Wagener', 'Lane's Prince Albert', 'Worcester Pearmain').

Pollination

Before a tree can bear fruit it is necessary for the blossom on it to be pollinated. Whilst some cultivars will set a crop with their own pollen, many will set no fruit at all unless fertilised by pollen of another cultivar. In planning the fruit garden, therefore, cultivars should be selected so that cross pollination may be ensured. Often neighbours' fruit trees will pro-

A large bush apple, suitable for large gardens where there is room for it to develop.

vide the necessary pollinators, but it is unwise to depend on this. Do not use any insecticides during the blossoming periods as they will kill hive bees and other pollinating insects.

Terms used in connection with fruit trees

At this stage it will be well to define briefly certain terms which are commonly used in connection with fruit tree culture.

MAIDEN: A one-year-old tree with a single straight stem. Sometimes there are side shoots and it is then known as a feathered maiden.

ROOTSTOCK: The plant on which fruits are grafted or budded (see p. 51) is commonly called 'rootstock' or 'stock'.

SCION: The shoot or bud of the cultivar which is grafted or

Left: A spindlebush apple.

Right: Young oblique cordons.

Below: Espalier apple—a useful decorative form.

budded on to the rootstock.

LEADER: The leading shoot or main growth of a branch. With a young tree the topmost growth is the leader.

BASAL CLUSTER. The closely spaced leaves at the base of an apple or pear shoot made in the current growing season.

LATERAL: A side growth or shoot arising from a branch or leader.

FRUIT OR BLOSSOM BUD: A bud which produces flowers. It is much fatter than the vegetative bud.

SPUR: A short growth bearing a fruit bud. Two or more spurs arising on the same growth combine to make what is known as a spur system.

SELF-STERILE OR SELF-INCOMPATIBLE: A term applied to cultivars which, before they can produce fruit, need to be fertilised with pollen from another cultivar.

SELF-FERTILE OR SELF-COMPATIBLE: Those cultivars of which the blossoms are capable of being fertilised with their own pollen.

Other special terms used are disbudding, thinning, pinching, incompatible, ringing, nicking, notching. These are explained below.

Shapes and forms of trees

The usual shapes in which fruit trees are grown are as follows:

BUSH. A stem of 2 or 3 feet (60 to 90 cm.) with branches arising fairly close together to form a head. Most top fruits can be grown successfully as bush trees and they are probably the most easily managed. It is not a suitable form for plums with drooping habit.

STANDARD AND HALF STANDARD. A main stem or trunk, 6 or 4 feet in height respectively (1.8 or 1.2 m.), at which point branches arise to form a large head. These trees are suitable for large plantations or orchards where there is plenty of room for them. They are too large for a small garden.

Espalier (left) and cordon (right) pears.

SPINDLEBUSH is a cone-shaped tree with a single vertical stem. The aim is to produce branches growing as nearly horizontal as possible, so encouraging fruiting. It is used for apples and, less commonly, pears.

Top fruits can also be grown in restricted forms against walls or in the open. By various methods of pruning and training, trees are induced to form certain shapes, and the growth of branches is restricted with the object of producing good quality fruit within a limited area. Summer pruning is an important part of the restricted systems of cultivation. The usual forms are as follows:

CORDON. A single straight stem on which side growths are restricted by pruning and which carries fruit spurs along its entire length. There are also double, triple and horizontal cordons. Cordon apples

Above: Dwarf pyramid apple: a useful form for a small garden.
Above, right: A fan-trained plum; also used for peach and cherry.

and pears are excellent for the small garden (see p. 65).

ESPALIER. A central main stem with pairs of more or less opposite branches growing out at right angles on each side. This is a very useful form in which to grow apples and pears (see p. 68).

FAN-TRAINED. A system of pruning and training branches upwards and outwards from the base – usually for growing a tree against a wall. Fruits often grown in this form are; plums, peaches, cherries, apricots and figs, but apples and pears will also do well (see p. 97).

PYRAMID AND DWARF PYR-AMID. A main stem from which, beginning at a little over a foot (30 cm.) from ground level, branches radiate at intervals in gradually diminishing length. Apples, pears and, with careful management, plums make successful pyramids (see p. 68–69).

Rootstocks

Apples, pears, plums and other cultivated tree fruits do not come true from seed. The usual means of perpetuating particular cultivars of these fruits is by uniting them, by methods known as budding and grafting, with a rootstock, which is in most cases a selected type of the fruit concerned. Budding and grafting are briefly described on pages 52–53.

The rootstocks for apples, pears and plums show considerable differences in habit of growth, vigour and rooting, and in their effect on the growth and character of the cultivar budded or grafted on them.

Source of supply

A Ministry of Agriculture Certification Scheme exists for certain tree fruits and covers many of the important cultivars of the apple, pear, plum and cherry. The scheme applies to the rootstocks, the source of scion material and the end product which is the fruit tree. Certified trees can be relied on to be free from stated viruses, substantially free from diseases and pests and true to name. Healthy trees crop more heavily than diseased ones and it will pay the grower to obtain certified trees wherever possible. In any event it is important to find out when buying trees what rootstocks have been used for grafting.

Propagation

As already mentioned, fruit trees are propagated either by budding or by grafting the cultivar selected on to the chosen rootstock.

Budding is usually done during July and early August, and grafting in March or April. The processes of budding and grafting are fully described in many textbooks, and are shown in the following pictures. Two methods of budding are shown, in one a T-shaped cut is used, and the

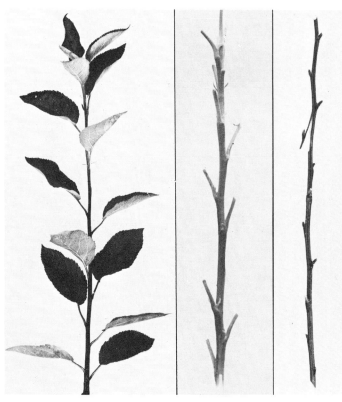

Left, above:
Buds are cut from a shoot of the current season's growth.
The leaf blades are cut off to leave about ½ in. (6 mm.) of stalk to serve as a handle when inserting the bud.
The bud is thinly sliced off the shoot with a sharp knife.

other is chip budding. The second has been shown to give a higher percentage of successful unions.

In grafting, a length of dormant one-year-old wood of the cultivar, some 3 or 4 buds long, known as the scion is united with the root-stock, which should have been planted one year before. The graft or union thus made is tied with raffia or plastic strip and all ex-posed surfaces are covered over with a 'grafting wax' or a proprietary bitumen emulsion sold for the purpose. The buds on the graft should start to grow a few weeks after it has been made and one of the shoots is trained up to form the maiden.

Left, below:
The bud is ready for insertion into the T-shaped cut on the stock.
The bud is slipped under the bark; and any part above the cross cut is trimmed off.

Right above:
In chip budding a wider cut is made in the stock.
The bud chip is placed over the cut. It is bound with polythene tape.
In February of the next year the rootstock above the bud is cut away.
Grafting
Right, below:
The scion (left) is prepared by making a flat sloping cut about 2 in. (5 cm.) long, and a downward pointing tongue made by an upward cut. In the rootstock the same cut is made but the tongue points upward. Both are brought together with the tongues interlocking, but the inner edge of the rind of both cuts must coincide on at least one side.
The union is tied with tape.
And cut surfaces are covered with grafting wax.

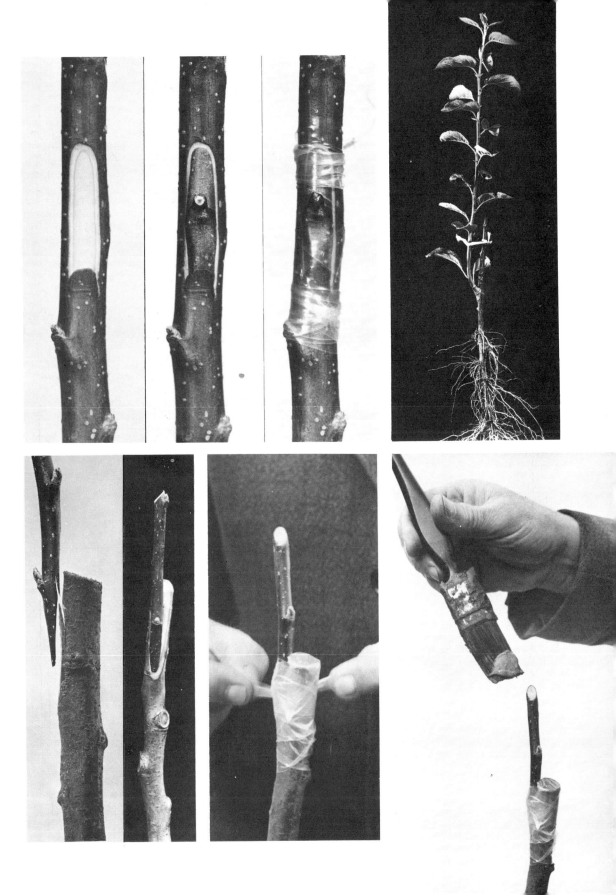

Above: when planting make sure that the union between stock and scion is at least 6 in. (15 cm.) above ground level; the finger points to ground level.

Right: tree after planting, showing the position of the union, the stake and the tie.

Planting

Many experienced growers like to plant their trees as maidens and then prune and train them in the form they want. Maidens are cheaper and usually grow away better than older trees but the beginner may prefer to buy a tree up to three years old which has already been shaped by the nurseryman. This is not advisable for apples on M.9, which should preferably be not more than two years old at planting, otherwise they may not become properly established by the time they start cropping.

Planting can be done at any time between November and March, provided weather and soil conditions are right, though early winter is to be preferred. Avoid planting when the ground is frozen or very wet. If planting cannot be done soon after the trees are delivered, the packing material should be removed from the roots and the trees at once 'heeled in'. This is done by digging a hole or trench, placing the roots in it and covering them with soil; they should be well firmed in (see p. 135). If the weather is frosty they should not be unpacked but kept in a frost-proof outbuilding. If the roots are dry, as may happen when the trees are delivered late, they should be soaked for about an hour before planting.

Before planting trim any damaged roots, making a long sloping cut on the underside. Dig a hole wide enough for the roots to be spread out comfortably; do not cramp them. The hole should not be too deep as it is most important that the union between stock and scion should be at least 4 inches (10 cm.) above soil level after planting. It is often possible to see on the stem where the soil came to in the nursery, and it is usually correct to plant to the same depth. Sufficient soil should be removed to allow the roots to rest comfortably on the convex-shaped bed of the hole. Replace the soil a spadeful at a time, moving the tree up and down to get the soil well round the roots and tread the soil firmly as the

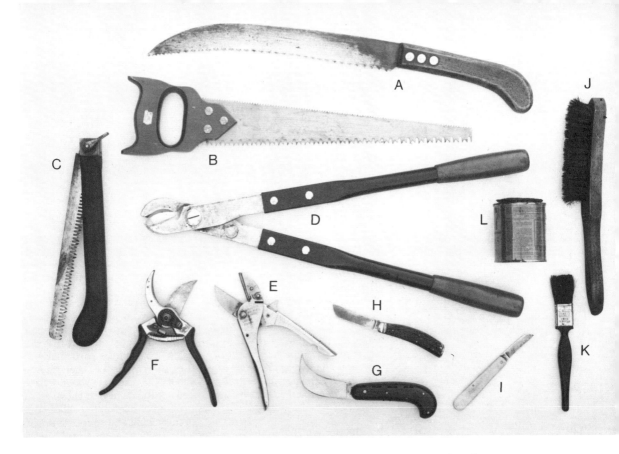

hole is filled in. Use the best top spit for putting round the roots. A barrow-load of sandy soil is useful for mixing in when planting in heavy ground. Remember that firm planting is essential for success. If rabbits or hares are troublesome protect stems with wire netting or a plastic guard.

Fruit trees will not thrive in poorly drained soils and ideally on such sites the drainage should be improved before planting. However on very heavy land, and in situations where the ground may lie wet during the winter and drainage cannot be improved, it is a good plan to make a shallow hole, piling up the soil round the roots and sloping it away from the main stem. In effect the tree is planted on a mound.

All trees should be staked at planting. A vertical stake, well driven in and planted with the tree, is the usual method and gives the firmest support, but oblique stakes are sometimes used. Use soft string for tying; a piece of

cloth wrapped round the trunk will prevent damage to the bark. Alternatively use a proprietary tree tie which provides a cushion between tree and stake. It is well to leave permanent tying until the soil has settled down, particularly on heavy soils. Tree ties should be checked annually to make sure that they are firm, but have not become too tight.

Pruning: general principles

Pruning is a most important operation in fruit culture and must be done as well as possible to obtain the best yields. The rootstock, soil, situation, climatic conditions and manuring also affect growth and consequently the pruning required.

The main reasons for pruning are:

1. to build the shape of the tree.
2. to encourage fruit bud formation and regulate the number and position of the fruit buds which develop.

Before starting any winter

Fruitgrower's tools.
A.B.C. Three types of pruning saw; A is useful for cutting out awkwardly placed branches; C is a folding saw. D long-handled pruners. E.F. two types of hand secateurs. G pruning knife. H grafting knife. I budding knife. J wire brush for cleaning up canker. K.L. brush and tin of bituminous paint.

pruning the habit of the tree and the position of the fruit buds should be noted. Different cultivars of apples and pears respond differently to similar pruning operations. Firm rules for pruning cannot be made, only certain methods recommended.

Cultivars of apples can be classified into two main classes in relation to cropping, the spur bearers and the tip bearers:

1. Those which produce fruit buds and spurs on relatively short growths called spurs close to the branch, e.g. 'Ellison's Orange', 'James Grieve', 'Cox's Orange Pippin'.

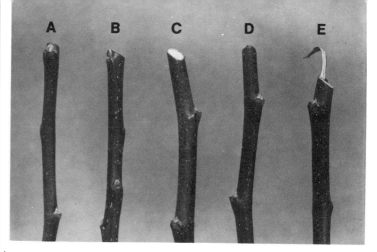

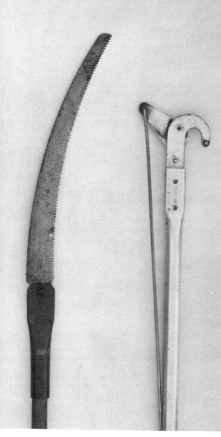

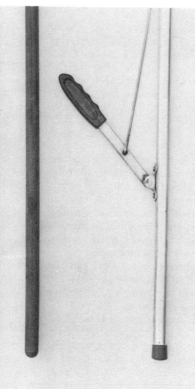

Left, a pole saw and right a long-arm pruner for tall trees.
Above:
Pruning cuts should be made close to the bud, as shown in A and B. Common faults are shown in C.D.E in all of which the cut has been made too far above the bud. In C the cut is also sloping the wrong way and in E a snag has been left, probably because the secateurs were blunt.

2. Those which produce fruit buds at or towards the tips of young shoots, e.g. 'Bramley's Seedling', 'Worcester Pearmain', 'Tydeman's Early'.

Because of these differences the treatment should not be the same in each case. Unless this tip-bearing habit is recognised and a good proportion of shoots left un-pruned, the fruit buds are likely to be pruned away each year, especially when the trees are young.

It is also necessary to know something of the tree's response to pruning; thus plum trees, except when grown against a wall, need little pruning once the head has been formed, except to cut away dead and diseased wood, but apple and pear trees should be pruned regularly throughout their lives if they are to make healthy growth and produce good quality fruit. Unpruned trees, though they may come into early cropping and for a year or two produce good quality fruit, lose vigour as time goes on and the fruit produced becomes poor in size and quality. They also tend to bear crops every other year (biennial bearing).

Winter pruning is done any time between leaf-fall and bud-burst. The harder a tree is winter pruned the more vigorously it will grow. This applies particularly to the shortening of the leading shoots (i.e. the new shoots at the ends of the main branches). Hard pruning of the leading shoots and of the laterals and spurs, especially with young trees, will delay cropping.

The amount of leader shortening and other pruning depends on the cultivar, age, vigour, condition and the form of tree.

Summer pruning, which consists of shortening the current season's growth (explained on p. 62) restricts growth and helps to maintain trees of a dwarf and compact habit.

APPLES

Apples are the most widely grown of the tree fruits and reasons for this are not hard to find. One cultivar or another will succeed in most parts of Britain and on most soils and can usually be counted on to crop satisfactorily, often heavily. There is an apple, dessert or culinary, for every taste and no other fruit can provide a range of cultivars during nine months of the year.

Given regular attention and providing one or two simple rules are observed, apple trees will remain healthy and fruitful for fifty years or longer. There are of course certain pitfalls to be avoided. In many older gardens there are still very large old trees but with the excellent dwarfing and semi-dwarfing rootstocks available for apples, there is no need to grow large trees. Picking, pruning and spraying of smaller trees can be easily done from the ground, or from household steps. The need for adequate cross pollination is vital, since without it the majority of cultivars will not crop satisfactorily (see pp. 118–119). Where space is limited choose high quality, late, dessert cultivars which can be stored and used over a long period; early apples will not keep and cookers are comparatively cheap to buy.

In favourable conditions a well-grown cordon in full bearing can produce as much as 10 lb. (4.5 kg.), or more, of fruit; but the amateur should be well satisfied with an average of 3 to 5 lb. (1.5 to 2.2 kg.). The figures for dwarf pyramids are 15 lb. (7 kg.) or more with an average of 6 to 8 lb. (2.7 to 3.6 kg.); and a bush tree on M.9, 60 lb. (27 kg.) or more with an average of 25 to 30 lb. (11.2 to 13.5 kg.), and a bush tree on M.2, 200 lb. (90 kg.) or more with an average of 80 to 100 lb. (36 to 45 kg.). The yield from an espalier will largely depend on the size of the tree, but it cannot be expected to give much more than half that of a bush tree on the same rootstock, and probably less.

Trees take a number of years to start fruiting, depending on stock, type of tree and method of pruning. A cordon should start fruiting within two years of planting, a dwarf pyramid within two to three years, and a bush tree on M.9 in its third year; but it may be 5 or 6 years before a bush tree on M.2 gives any appreciable crop. A cordon can yield a good crop of fruit when 4 to 5 years old.

Rootstocks
Rootstocks are classified according to their effect on the growth of the cultivar. By budding or grafting the cultivar on a certain rootstock, it is now possible within reasonable limits to forecast the size that trees are likely to reach and how soon they will fruit.

Certain apple rootstocks are specially suitable for the produc-

Sixteen-year-old bush trees of 'Worcester Pearmain' showing the effect of rootstock on tree size. Top, on M.2; centre, on M.9; below, on M.7.

tion of early cropping, compact trees which are ideal for the small garden. These include Malling Nos. 9, 26 and Malling-Merton 106.

The choice of rootstock must be related to the type of soil and the form of tree required. M.9 is the most dwarfing rootstock and trees on this stock may start bearing fruit after only 2 or 3 years. M.26, a comparatively new stock, is a little more vigorous. The two semi-dwarfing stocks M.7 and MM.106 are roughly equal in vigour and produce medium sized trees. Cultivars on M.2 or MM. 111 come into bearing later and make large trees on good loamy soils, but only medium-sized trees in poorer sandy soils.

Bush Tree
This is the most easily managed form of tree.

ROOTSTOCKS AND SPACING
M.9 (dwarfing) is generally the best choice for a small garden, but is not suitable for poor conditions. Trees require a permanent stake. Plant at 8 to 10 feet (2.5 to 3 m.) apart.
M.26 (dwarfing) is slightly more vigorous. Trees require firm staking. Plant at 10 to 15 feet (3 to 4.5 m.) apart.
M.7 and MM.106 (semi-dwarfing). On relatively poor soils MM.106 can be used for obtaining dwarf or small trees instead of M.9. Plant at 12 to 18 feet (3.5 to 5.5 m.) apart.

WINTER PRUNING OF YOUNG TREES
Maiden Trees. First winter: after planting cut back to 20 or 24 inches (50 to 60 cm.). Second winter: select up to 4 of the result-ant growths for branch leaders, shorten these by about $\frac{1}{2}$ to $\frac{2}{3}$, to outward-pointing buds.

Ten-year-old trees of 'Bramley Seedling' on (top) a vigorous stock (M.12) unsuitable for small gardens, and bearing a very poor crop; (below) M.9. a dwarfing rootstock suitable for small gardens.

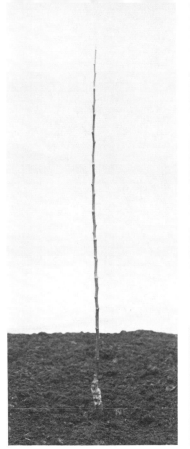
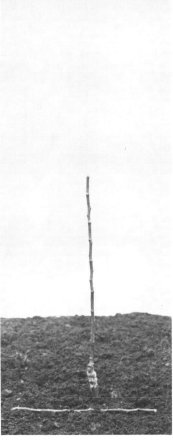

Above, left to right:
Newly planted maiden.
Cut back to 24 in. (60 cm.).
The next winter, before pruning.

Below:
After pruning: the new shoots selected as leaders have been cut back by two-thirds.
The following winter: the three-year-old tree before pruning.

Older Trees. After planting cut back leaders by $\frac{1}{2}$ to $\frac{2}{3}$ of length. *Note:* If planted very late or if growth conditions are likely to be poor, leave them unpruned in the first season and cut back into two-year-old wood next winter.

Subsequently, the leading shoots require shortening according to the growth the tree is making. With trees on M.9 between one-third is removed if the tree is growing vigorously, to two-thirds, if it is weakly. The leaders of trees on stronger stocks require less shortening.

In the early years some of the

Above left to right:
After pruning. The leading shoots have been cut back by about two-thirds; laterals to about three buds. The following winter: a four-year-old tree before pruning.
Below, left:
The same tree after pruning. The leaders have been shortened by a third, and the laterals cut back to about three buds.

longer shoots on the outside and lower part of the tree can be left unpruned. These will usually produce spurs and can then be shortened.

As the tree gets older it will be necessary to thin out the spurs from time to time or they will become too congested.

Bush trees can also be pruned in the summer (see p. 62).

Half-standard and Standard Trees

Both the half-standard and standard are grafted on to vigorous stocks and eventually make large

to very large trees. They are not, therefore, suitable for the average sized garden. In time both will outcrop the smaller bush tree but they will take longer to come into cropping and being larger will require more effort in spraying, pruning and picking.

The pruning of the half-standard and standard is basically the same as for the bush tree except for the initial formative pruning. The half standard has a clean stem of about 4 to 4½ feet (1.2 to 1.4 m.) and at this height the main framework or head arises. The standard has a clean stem of about 6 feet (1.8 m.).

INITIAL PRUNING

Most maiden apple trees are not tall enough to head back at 4½ feet (1.4 m.) or 6½ feet (2 m), and it will be necessary to run them on to the two year stage to reach the necessary height. During this period they should be trained up a six or eight foot (1.8 to 2.4 m.) cane. All laterals should be left

Pruning a tip-bearing cultivar (see p. 56). Before pruning; after pruning. The lateral at the top right arising from the main branch has been cut back to three buds. Most of the shoots from laterals have been cut back to one bud; some shoots have not been pruned so that they will develop fruit buds at their tips. The leader has been shortened by about half.

intact during the first two growing seasons to help to thicken the trunk. Vigorous laterals should be pinched at six leaves. The leader is left unpruned.

In the second winter after planting tip the leader back to a bud at 4½ feet (1.4 m.) for a half-standard or 6½ feet (2 m.). for a standard. Thereafter follow the same principles as for the bush tree. See pages 58–60. All laterals should be removed below the main framework once the tree has formed a stout trunk. Protect pruning cuts with a bitumen tree paint.

Winter pruning of established trees

Apart from the formation and maintenance of a tree of the desired shape with well-spaced branches, the less pruning there is the more quickly fruit buds will develop. By cutting back the shoots of a tree in the dormant season, the growth of buds beneath the cut is stimulated; the harder the pruning the stronger the shoots produced.

The art of winter pruning lies in the removal of unprofitable growths (which if left would result in the tree becoming a tangled mass) in order that good quality fruit is produced, the cutting back of other growths for the production of new wood and the regulation of the number of fruit buds allowed to develop.

By pruning a *young* tree in the dormant season it is possible to control its shape. An *established* tree is pruned in the winter to regulate growth, maintain the shape and cropping power as well as to improve fruit quality.

An established tree is one of four years old or older and the type of growth and the manner in which its fruit buds are borne will be apparent. Cultivars differ considerably in these characteristics.

With most apple cultivars the buds at or near the base of one-year-old laterals (i.e. last season's growth), will tend to remain dormant in spring if left unpruned in the previous winter, whilst those towards the end will break into growth; thus an appreciable part of each lateral will often remain bare. For this reason the laterals are shortened during the dormant season, so encouraging the formation of fruiting buds and spurs close to the branch on which the laterals arise. Summer pruning, referred to later, also has a modifying effect. This treatment of the laterals can be repeated annually, cutting back to a fruit bud, if desirable, when one has formed.

When pruning branch *leaders*, it is important with young estab-

lished trees to remember the need to stimulate the production of branches strong enough to carry the weight of future crops. Consequently for a few years after the framework of the tree has been laid down it may be advisable to shorten some of the leaders by about one quarter. Growth will then be stimulated from buds lower down, and stout young side branches will be built up. Later on it may be necessary to tip the leaders lightly, and some may be left unpruned. With most cultivars leaders that are not pruned or only lightly tipped, will produce fruit buds on two-year-old wood. In due course – with trees whose growth is not to be restricted – all the winter pruning necessary, apart from the removal of unwanted growths, will be the shortening of the laterals as described above and the tipping of some of the leaders. When pruning leaders bear in mind the growth habit of the tree. With a cultivar that produces spreading

Pruning a spur-bearing cultivar (see p. 56). Before and after pruning. Laterals have been cut back to three or four buds; shoots from laterals pruned in the previous year have been cut back to one bud. The leader has been shortened.

growth, such as 'Beauty of Bath', the leaders are pruned to an inward-pointing bud to encourage more erect growth. With an upright-growing cultivar such as 'Worcester Pearmain' and 'Chiver's Delight' prune the leaders to an outward-pointing bud to encourage more spreading growth.

As the trees increase in size, thin out any branches which touch or cross. Remove them close to the main stem and with large branches cut them off in two pieces for ease of handling. Undercut if necessary to avoid any risk of stripping the bark as the branch falls. Pare down all saw cuts with a sharp knife and seal with a bituminous paint. Any branches which are too vigorous and spoiling the balance of the tree should also be removed. This will let light and air into the centre of the tree.

Spur systems which have become crowded should be thinned out from time to time by the removal of some and the cutting back of others to reduce the clusters of fruit buds. Laterals which may then grow can be developed into fruiting wood forming strong spurs.

After some years, in order that the tree may be maintained in good shape, low hanging leaders are best removed, allowing well-placed laterals to take their place. These are known as replacement leaders.

SUMMER PRUNING
Summer pruning is not needed during the first years for trees grown in an unrestricted form. It may sometimes be used with advantage, however, once a young tree starts to crop but it is not essential for bush trees. The

benefit obtained from summer pruning is based partly on the fact that the removal of foliage during the summer checks root action and consequently shoot growth. It also encourages the development of fruit buds near the base of the pruned shoots. By the removal of superfluous growths, light and air are admitted to a tree, resulting in well-ripened wood and buds, and well-coloured fruits.

In its simplest form summer pruning consists of cutting back, to some 5 in. (12 cm.) from their point of origin, those laterals of current season's growth which have become woody at the base. Do not prune all at once, start with some of the longer laterals early in August and complete the operation during September. *Do not summer prune the leaders.*

Summer pruning of trees grown in a restricted form is necessary for their training and maintenance. The summer pruning of other trees may be beneficial in

producing well-coloured fruits.

If a tree is not growing well it should not be summer pruned.

Spindlebush
Basically the spindlebush is a cone-shaped tree. It consists of a central stem from which starting at about 2 ft (60 cm.) above ground level branches or cropping laterals grow uniformly spaced along its length. The three or four lowest branches are usually regarded as permanent and carry a herringbone system of cropping laterals pruned on the renewal method. The upper branches are kept shorter than the lower branches so that the cone shape is maintained. These are not regarded as permanent but are cut out whenever they become too crowded, too dominant or unproductive. The top laterals are treated as cropping laterals to be stubbed back to about 1 in. (2.5 cm.) after cropping. Tying down the branches and cropping laterals is practised to obtain nearly

Pruning Leaders
Above left, an apple with a spread-ing habit ('Beauty of Bath').

Above right, an apple with an erect habit ('Chiver's Delight').

horizontal growth. The trees are supported by an 8 to 9 feet (2.5 m. – 3 m.) pole. Because of the pole and the string needed for tying, the spindle cannot be regarded as aesthetically pleasing. Neverthe-less this tree shape allows plenty of sunlight to reach the lower branches and this factor together with the wide angle of the laterals is conducive to fruitfulness. Quite heavy crops of well coloured fruits are obtained by commercial growers using this method.

Spur Thinning
Left, part of a branch on which the spurs have become crowded.

Right, the same branch after the removal of some spurs and the thinning out of others.

Branch of an apple tree before summer pruning in August.

The same branch after summer pruning.

ROOTSTOCKS AND SPACING
M.9 (dwarfing)

M.26 or MM.106, on poor soils

On M.9 or in poor soils on M.26, plant at 6 to 7 feet (2 m.) between the trees and 12 feet (3.5 m.) between the rows.

On M.26 or MM.106 on good soils allow at least 7½ to 8½ feet (2 to 2.5 m.) between the trees and 14 feet (4.5 m.) between the rows.

STAKING
The stakes should be 8 to 8½ feet (2.5 m.) long of which 1½ to 2 feet (45 to 60 cm.) is buried. They should be treated with preservative and have a minimum top diameter of 1¾ in. (4.5 cm.).

PRUNING
In the *first winter* cut back a maiden tree to a bud at 3 feet (90 cm.) high. For a feathered maiden, choose 3 or 4 well placed feathers (laterals) not less than 2 feet (60 cm.) from the ground to make the first tier of branches and cut these back by half to a downward pointing bud. Remove the remainder. Cut back the central stem to 2 buds above the top lateral chosen as a branch.

By August if growing conditions have been good a number of laterals should have grown from the main stem. If these growths are vigorous start tying down laterals to form wide-angled branches. If growth is moderate to weak tying down may be delayed until the second summer. The 3 or 4 laterals chosen should form naturally wide angles with the main stem to encourage even growth. The correct angle to tie the branches down is 30° above the horizontal using fairly thick string secured to pegs or skewers in the ground. Any upright laterals and those directly beneath the central leader should be removed.

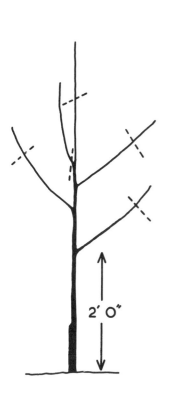

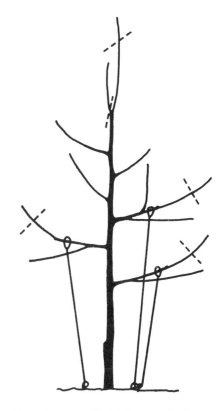

Spindlebush
Left, one-year-old feathered maiden at planting: centre, one-year-old unfeathered maiden, at planting: right, second-year pruning of feathered maiden, the main branches are tied down. The broken lines indicate the position of the pruning cut.

In the second winter, cut back the central upright leader by about one third or more if the growth is weak, to a bud on the opposite side to that of the previous year. Remove any shoots directly below which are competing with the central leader, and any other vigorous upright shoots on the tree. Laterals needed for branches should be lightly tipped. Check the ties to make sure they are not too tight and remove any where the branches have set at the required angle.

Further tying down of suitable laterals to form branches should be done in August.

In the third and subsequent years, to stimulate the production of more laterals, the central leader should again be pruned, the amount depending on its vigour. The more vigorous the leader is the less it is pruned. Branches are allowed to grow from the central leader at regular intervals choosing wide-angled shoots; those with narrow angles are removed completely. The higher placed branches must be kept shorter than the lower ones to allow plenty of light to reach the lower parts, while those at the top of the tree are treated as fruiting laterals to be cut back after cropping and so are not tipped. Throughout the life of the tree a balanced proportion of maiden and fruiting laterals is kept by light renewal pruning. Once the central leader has reached its allotted height of 7 to 8 ft (2 to 2.5 m.) the extension growth is cut back annually to a weaker side branch which is tied to the stake.

Tying down is important in the early years to achieve a balance between fruitfulness and vigour. Once the tree is cropping the need for tying down becomes less.

Cordon
ROOTSTOCKS AND SPACING
M.9 (dwarfing) is a good stock for most cultivars.
M.26 (dwarfing).
M.7 and MM.106 (semi-dwarfing) are good for some cultivars that do not produce laterals and spur freely.
M.2 and MM.111 (vigorous) are good for any cultivar where soil is poor.

Plant trees at $2\frac{1}{2}$–3 feet (75 to 90 cm.) apart, the rows not less than 6 feet (1.8 m.) apart. The wider spacing is suggested for shallow or sandy soils.

SUPPORT
A permanent system of wiring as described below is necessary. Posts of iron, steel, concrete or wood (thoroughly impregnated with preservative) are set at 12 foot (3.5 m.) intervals with 7 feet (2 m.)

of post above ground level, and with 3 parallel wires stretched between the posts. The bottom wire should be stretched tightly at a height of $2\frac{1}{2}$ feet (75 cm.) above soil level and the others at 2 feet (60 cm.) intervals. If the posts are set in concrete they should be 18 in. (45 cm.) below ground or if in soil 3 feet (90 cm.) below making a total length of $8\frac{1}{2}$ (2.6 m.) or 10 feet (3.2 m.) respectively. The top wire should be gauge 10, the lower wires can be 12 or 13. Stranded wire is preferable. As the wires must be tight it is as well to use adjustable straining bolts at the end posts and the posts must be suitably strutted. Bamboo canes 8 to 10 feet (2.5 to 3.2 m.) long are tied to the wires with wire or strong string and the cordons are trained along them. The ties between tree and cane require

Cordon end posts suitably strutted.

Newly planted oblique cordons secured to canes. Note that the scion has been planted uppermost.

Young cordons in July, before pruning.

The same cordons after pruning.

periodical examination and renewal. Cordons can also be grown against fences or walls. Here too they need the support of canes and wires.

PLANTING

It is best to plant maidens if obtainable. Cordons can be grown vertically where there is adequate height, but it is better to plant them at an angle of 45° to the soil level. Plant with the scion part of the union uppermost to reduce risk of breakage and scion rooting. Rows should run north and south, if possible, to facilitate even growth, with the leader pointing north. For general directions as to planting see pp. 54–55.

PRUNING AND TRAINING

Maiden tree: No pruning is necessary after planting although tip-bearing cultivars should have the leader pruned back by one quarter. If there are 'feathers' (i.e. side shoots) those more than 4 in. (10 cm.) long should be shortened to three buds during the winter. Thereafter prune in summer.

A system of summer pruning (with no regular winter pruning) usually gives the best results in most districts. The following method, the Modified Lorette System, can be generally recommended. It has been found satisfactory for all cultivars and is best for tip bearers.

About mid-July in southern England (later further north) cut back all mature laterals growing directly from the main stem to three leaves beyond the basal cluster, and those from existing side shoots or spurs to one leaf. If there are only a few immature shoots treat them in the same way; but if there are many leave them until mid-September and then prune them. Mature shoots are those 9 in. (23 cm.) or more long,

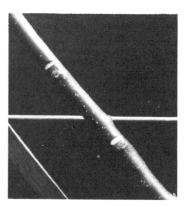

Left: Some apples tend to produce bare lengths of stem unless carefully leader-tipped. This can be avoided by notching, either when pruning in winter or later when it is noticed that a particular bud is not growing.

Above: A crescent-shaped chip of bark is cut out immediately above the bud.

with a woody base and dark leaves.

There is sometimes secondary growth in late summer from shoots pruned in July; cut them back in October to one bud.

The pruning of secondary growth must be completed by the early winter as the immature wood is susceptible to cold injury, leading possibly to the entry of disease.

When cordons reach the top wire they should be loosened and lowered. To avoid having to do this every year do not lower less than 5° at a time. Keep them parallel with their neighbours.

Do not shorten the leader unless the tree has become too long. It should then be cut back to the desired length in May. But if space is restricted and the tree is not producing sufficient side shoots, the leader may be shortened in the winter by up to one third of its length, although this will delay cropping. Any necessary thinning of spurs should also be done in the winter.

NOTCHING

The removal of a small portion of bark immediately above a latent bud has the effect of stimulating it into growth. With cordons and other restricted trees it is sometimes desirable to do this in May, so preventing bare lengths of stem. Notching is also of use when the shape of a young tree is being formed. It is often used in conjunction with 'nicking', which consists of cutting the bark immediately *below* a bud. This results in a weaker growth from that bud than would otherwise be the case.

Espalier

ROOTSTOCKS

M.9 (dwarfing) is only suitable if a small tree is required, e.g. if planted against a low fence. Plant 10 feet (3.2 m.) apart.

M.26 (dwarfing) is slightly more vigorous than M.9. Plant 10 to 12 feet (3.2–3.5 m.) apart.

M.7 and MM.106 (semi-dwarfing) are suitable for medium sized

trees. Plant 12 to 15 feet (3.5–4.5 m.) apart.

M.2 and MM.111 (vigorous) are the most useful stocks for large espaliers. Plant 15 to 18 feet (4.5–5.5 m.) apart.

PRUNING

The pruning of espaliers in the formative and later years is described under pears (see pp. 84–86). However as apple growth is later to mature than pear, summer pruning is done about mid July in southern England (later further north).

Dwarf Pyramid

ROOTSTOCKS AND SPACING

M.9 (dwarfing) is a little too dwarfing for most cultivars.

M.26 is dwarfing, but more vigorous than M.9.

M.7 and MM.106 (semi-dwarfing) are satisfactory for most cultivars.

M.2 and MM.111 (vigorous) are suitable where growth conditions are unfavourable, otherwise too vigorous.

Plant at 4–5 feet (1.2–1.5 m.) apart in rows and preferably 7 feet (2 m.) apart between rows.

A corner of a plot of dwarf pyramid apples: note the spacing of 4–5 ft (1.2–1.5 m.) between the trees and 7 ft (2 m.) between the rows.

Maidens are best if obtainable. Trees on M.9 and probably M.26 must be supported throughout their life. Support can be provided by running two strands of wire down the rows, fastened to posts at intervals of about 15 feet (4.5 m.), at about 18 in. (45 cm.) and 3 feet (90 cm.) above ground level, the trees being tied to the wires.

PRUNING

The pruning of dwarf pyramids is described in detail under pears (pp. 82–83). But as apple growth is later to mature than pear, summer pruning is done about mid-July in southern England (later further north).

Establishment of a grass sward

Commercially apples are planted in arable land and the age at which they are grassed down depends largely on the types of trees being grown, their vigour and other factors such as the soil and its water supply.

Trees grown in restricted form or on dwarfing stocks are usually grassed down early in life, generally in the second, third or fourth year after planting. Bush or larger trees are grassed down in their fifth or sixth years. For closely planted trees it is sufficient to limit the sward to the centre 3 feet (90 cm.) between the rows. At a wider spacing each tree should have an area of not less than 2½ feet (75 cm.) radius of clear land around the stem, but if the trees are growing very vigorously then the whole orchard can be grassed down. However do not allow the grass to grow right up to the tree trunk as damp conditions round the stem could favour the fungal disease, collar rot.

Fine grasses should generally be used, as it has been found that coarse grasses tend to restrict growth too much. A suitable mixture is 1½ oz. (50 g.) rough stalked meadow grass and ¼ oz. (9 g.) wild white clover, sown over 10 sq. yds (10 sq.m.).

The grass should be kept almost as short as a lawn during the growing season, the mowings being left lying. More nitrogen will have to be applied to trees growing in grass than to those in cultivated soil.

The check to vegetative growth caused by grassing down may be of value in inducing trees to crop but an excessive check could be detrimental to both growth and fruit size. Cooking apples are usually best grown in arable conditions.

Manuring

For general principles see p. 9.

Potash is essential to apples and should be properly balanced with nitrogen. Each year in late February apply 1 oz. (33 g.) of sulphate of ammonia plus ¾ oz. (25 g.)

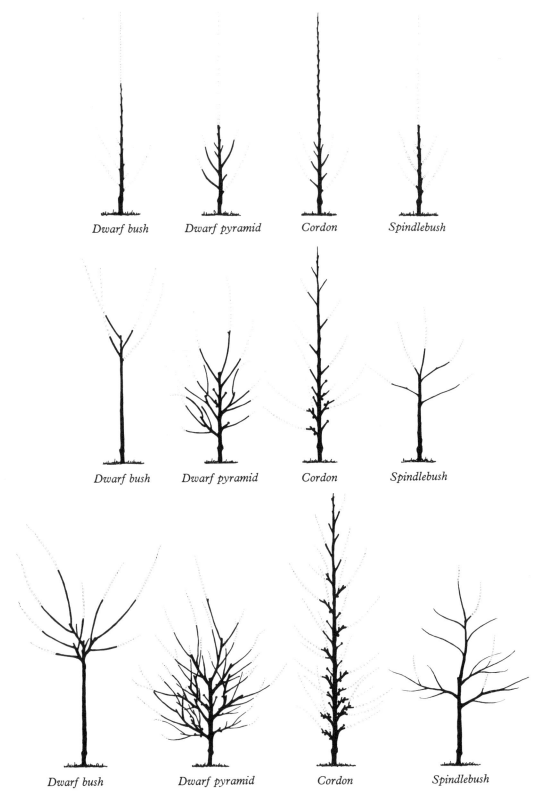

Dwarf bush Dwarf pyramid Cordon Spindlebush

Dwarf bush Dwarf pyramid Cordon Spindlebush

Dwarf bush Dwarf pyramid Cordon Spindlebush

Left: Methods of pruning for a dwarf bush, a dwarf pyramid, a cordon and a spindlebush, starting from a one-year-old tree.

sulphate of potash per sq. yard (sq. m.). Every 2 or 3 years apply 1½ to 2 oz. superphosphate per sq. yard (50 to 66 g. per sq. m.). Trees in grass should be given an extra oz. (per sq. yd) of sulphate of ammonia annually. Cooking apples can be given a little more nitrogen than dessert cultivars. An occasional dressing of farmyard manure or compost, especially where the land is not in good heart, will be beneficial, but too much farmyard manure is not good for apples.

Fruit thinning

There are considerable differences in the cropping habits of apple cultivars. Some are known as light bearers, others are naturally heavy croppers. Again, some normally bear a heavy crop every alternate year, whilst others crop annually.

When a tree is carrying a very heavy crop the fruit is usually small and of poor quality. The size and quality of the individual fruits can be greatly improved by thinning, though the total weight may not always be as heavy as the unthinned crop.

Bearing a heavy crop puts a big strain upon the tree. Thinning will relieve this. A young tree which is allowed to crop too freely, is likely to be set back in its growth and takes time to recover. Biennial bearing may also be induced. A heavy crop will also often result in broken branches and thinning will help to prevent this. Much depends on the cultivar, age and condition of the tree; for instance, trees growing vigorously with strong healthy foliage are capable of supporting a heavier crop than those that are weakly, and the fruit on these can well be left closer than on the latter.

Sharp scissors (such as vine scissors) may be used to cut the stalks. Alternatively, the fruits can be removed by gripping the stalk between the first two fingers and pressing the fruit off with the thumb; the stalk is left on the tree. If the young fruits are in a tight cluster, twist the one to be removed until it leaves the stalk.

Most apple cultivars – including 'Cox's Orange' – shed fruitlets naturally towards the end of June and early July in what is known as the 'June drop', but some extra thinning may be required. A little can be done before June drop takes place, by removing the malformed fruits, and the balance afterwards.

On large bush trees it is advisable to space the fruits out well. With some cultivars it may be necessary to thin to about 4 to 6 in. (10 to 15 cm.) apart to get a good proportion of apples of size 2½ to 2¾ in. (6.5 to 7 cm.) in

Right, above: The king apple is usually removed. Left: Then small or misshapen fruits. Right: One or two of the best fruitlets from a truss are left to develop.

Maypoling: a stake driven close to the tree forms a support for the branches to be tied to.

diameter. Similarly, to get fruits of the large cooking cultivars of say 3 to 3¼ in. (7.5 to 8 cm.) in diameter, the fruit must be spaced from 6 to 9 in. (15 to 23 cm.) apart.

With cordons and dwarf trees on M.9, the fruits are usually larger and heavy thinning is seldom necessary. Dessert cultivars can be thinned to singles. If the fruit is sparse then doubles can be left. With some cultivars, such as 'Ellison's Orange', 'Laxton's Superb' and 'Charles Ross', the fruit may grow too big if reduced to singles and, therefore, a good proportion of doubles should be left.

Most cooking apples are thinned to singles. For large specimens of 'Early Victoria' the fruit will have to be spaced well apart.

Besides blemished and misshapen fruit the 'king' or 'crown' apple produced from the central flower of the blossom cluster is usually removed. Certain cultivars typically long-stalked e.g. 'Golden Delicious', produce normal-shaped king fruits and these may be left. Poorly shaped fruits do not store well.

Supporting heavily-laden branches
The weight of fruit on heavily-laden branches, even where thinned, may be great and cause breakages. Such branches need support. Forked stakes can be used to prop up individual branches, weak branches can be tied with string or webbing to stronger ones; hooked wires are sometimes used. A stake may be driven into the ground close to the stem of the tree, or fastened to the stem, and individual branches tied up to the top of the stake in maypole fashion.

Protection from birds
Birds can be very troublesome in late summer in pecking fruit.

Other than netting the tree, bags made of paper, polythene or muslin, or cones of newspaper, are valuable for protection. These should be wrapped round the fruits before they begin to colour or to ripen. Black cotton wound in and out of the branches or various proprietary bird scarers will also help.

Picking
Ripening varies with season and locality, so definite dates for the picking of the different cultivars cannot be given. The best test of readiness for picking is to lift the fruit gently and give it a very slight twist. If it parts easily from the spur, it is ready for picking. Fruits picked when immature may fail to ripen and will never develop their full flavour. If gathered too late the keeping quality may be reduced. But it is best to pick early apples slightly immature as they quickly go mealy on the tree.

All the apples on a tree do not ripen at the same time and it is best to clear them in two or three pickings. Highly coloured fruits, and those at the top of the tree, are usually ready first, then those at the sides, and lastly the shaded fruits in the middle. The dropping of apples is usually a sign that the time for picking is approaching. Although early-maturing apples must not be left on the tree too long, very late-keeping cultivars such as 'Granny Smith', 'Sturmer Pippin' and 'Wagener', are best left on the trees as long as birds and winter gales permit.

Fruit must be picked and handled with the greatest care. As the fruit is picked, it should be placed carefully in baskets, pails or similar receptacles, lined with paper or other protective material, being transferred with equal care to larger receptacles as necessary.

Right: The fruit is picked with care. Below: Very late keeping cultivars are left on the tree as long as possible, but not in severe frost.

Fruits should never be thrown or dropped into a container.

Storing the fruit

Apples and pears are the only top fruits that can be stored by the amateur for any length of time. Early apples and pears are not stored and it is seldom worth while taking elaborate steps to store mid-season cultivars as these only keep for a short length of time.

Keep fruit away from anything that will taint it, such as creosote, fresh paint, fertilisers, strong-smelling wood and damp, dirty hay or straw.

The late cultivars, however, only mature some time after picking and need to be stored for periods varying from 4 to 5 weeks to several months, according to cultivar, before they reach their full flavour and are ready to eat.

Unless there are large quantities of fruit to be dealt with there is no need for a specially built fruit room or an elaborate system of shelves and trays.

Apples will keep in excellent condition if wrapped in oiled wraps specially made or in newspaper cut to a convenient size and then placed in slatted wooden boxes so that there is ventilation.

Left: Apples may also be wrapped individually in oiled 'wraps'. Below, left: Fold two opposite corners over the fruit. Below: Fold over the other two corners. Below, right: Lay the wrapped fruit on a tray.

Apples wrapped in perforated plastic bags and ready for storage, on trays or in boxes.

Commercial apple boxes which sometimes can be obtained from greengrocers are ideal, but any wooden containers should be cleaned and sterilised between seasons. The fruit should be stored in a cool, frost and rodent proof place, such as a cellar or even a garden shed in a shady position. They can also be stored in polythene bags (150 gauge); these are left unsealed or pinholes are made to provide ventilation. This simple method prevents shrivelling and keeps the fruit clean.

Fruits will keep best in a moist atmosphere and a fairly low, even temperature; 40°F (4.5°C.) or just below is ideal but it is seldom possible to maintain this in England. They should not be stored in a loft, attic or any place where the air is likely to be warm and dry, or where they are subject

to draught and wide fluctuations of temperature.

Keep apples which ripen at different times in separate containers. If they can be removed from the store as they approach ripeness so much the better, especially if the store is an enclosed one, as ripening apples give off volatile substances which may cause other cultivars to ripen prematurely. If possible apples and pears are best stored separately.

Only sound fruit, with the stalk retained, should be stored. So long as the skin is not punctured or bruised, and the fruit is not scabby, it will usually store satisfactorily.

If there is a considerable quantity of fruit it is a good thing to grade it roughly for size, as often the larger fruits will be found to keep for a shorter time than the smaller ones and will need to be used first. The fruit will require looking over periodically, as no rotting fruit must be allowed to remain in the store.

Recommended cultivars

Cross pollination is required in most apple cultivars. Reference should be made to the pollination groups before a final choice is made. See pages 118–119.

DESSERT

George Cave, *mid-Aug*
Discovery, *mid-Aug to mid-Sep*
Owen Thomas★, *late Aug to early Sep*
Epicure★, *mid-Aug to mid-Sep*
Worcester Pearmain, *early Sep to early Oct*
James Grieve, *early Sep to mid-Oct*
Fortune★, *Sep to Oct*
St Edmund's Pippin★, *late Sep to Oct*
Ellison's Orange, *Sep to Oct*
Merton Beauty, *Sep to Oct*
Lord Lambourne, *late Sep to mid-Nov*

★ Good flavour.
† In small gardens grow on M.9 or M.26, but for trees of restricted shape such as espalier, M.9 is preferable.

Merton Charm, *Sep to Nov*
Mother (American Mother)★, *Oct to Dec*
Egremont Russet★, *Oct to Dec*
Gravenstein★†, *Oct to Dec*
Margil★, *Oct to Jan*
Ribston Pippin★, *Oct to Jan*
Sunset★, *Nov to Dec*
Chivers Delight, *Nov to Jan*
Kidd's Orange Red★, *Nov to Jan*
Cox's Orange Pippin★, *Nov to Jan*
Christmas Pearmain, *Nov to Jan*
Orleans Reinette★, *Nov to Jan*
Spartan, *Nov to Jan*
Superb (Laxton's), *Nov to Feb*
Ashmead's Kernel★, *Dec to Feb*
Claygate Pearmain★, *Dec to Feb*
Suntan†, *Dec to Mar*
Crispin†, *Dec to Feb*
Wagener, *Dec to Apr*
Idared, *Dec to Apr*
Duke of Devonshire★, *Jan to Mar*
Pixie★, *Jan to Mar*
Sturmer Pippin★, *Jan to Apr*
Tydeman's Late Orange★, *Dec to Apr*

CULINARY

Emneth Early (Early Victoria), *late July to mid-Aug*
Grenadier, *Aug to Sep*
George Neal★, *late Aug to early Oct*
Rev. W. Wilks, *late Aug to Nov*
Golden Noble★, *Sep to Jan*
Warner's King, *late Sep to Feb*
Howgate Wonder, *Oct to Jan*
Blenheim Orange★†, *Nov to Jan; an excellent dual purpose cultivar.*
Bramley's Seedling★†, *Nov to Feb*
Newton Wonder★†, *Nov to Mar*
Wellington★, *Nov to Mar*
Woolbrook Russet★, *Nov to Apr*
Lane's Prince Albert, *Dec to Mar*
Crawley Beauty, *Dec to Mar*
Monarch, *Dec to Mar*
Edward VII, *Dec to Apr*
Encore★, *Dec to Apr*
Annie Elizabeth, *Dec to June*

NEW CULTIVARS OF PROMISE

Katja, *Sep to Oct*
Gala, *Oct to Dec*
Greensleeves, *Oct to Nov*

FREEZING

Bramley's Seedling, Blenheim Orange, Encore, have proved satisfactory.

Pests

CODLING MOTH caterpillars are the main cause of maggoty apples. Eggs are laid on leaves in June and July and the caterpillars tunnel into the fruits. In mid-August they finish feeding, leave the fruits, and seek the protection of loose bark, or tree ties in which they spin cocoons and spend the winter.

Chemical control is difficult, especially on larger trees, but if adequate spraying equipment is available, infestations may be reduced by spraying fenitrothion or malathion four weeks after petal-fall (about mid-June) and again three weeks later to kill the caterpillars before they enter the fruits.

The overwintering caterpillars are sometimes trapped by tying sacking or corrugated cardboard bands around the trunks and branches in July and then removing them and destroying the caterpillars during the winter. Such measures are only likely to have an appreciable effect on subsequent infestations if practised rigorously over a fairly large area.

APPLE SAWFLY caterpillars also tunnel in fruits but they attack earlier in the season than codling moths and infested fruits fall off the trees by June. The caterpillars overwinter in the soil so that surface cultivation may disturb and kill them. Malathion or BHC applied immediately after petal-fall will kill the caterpillars, if applied thoroughly. Picking and destroying infested fruits in June will also help to limit later attacks.

APPLE APHIDS of four species infest buds, young shoots and leaves, and occasionally damage young fruits. Eggs overwinter on the trees and hatch from March onwards. A fifth species, the woolly aphid, overwinters as young aphids, not as eggs, and causes galls on the woody stems and branches.

Thorough spraying with tar oil in late December or early January kills over-wintering eggs and

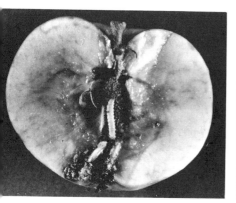

spraying with malathion, dimethoate or formothion in the pre-blossom period will check initial infestations. Woolly aphid colonies may be spot-treated by brushing in a spray-strength solution of BHC, malathion, dimethoate or formothion or by applying one or other of these insecticides as a drenching spray after flowering is over.

APPLE SUCKERS are related to aphids but are more flattened in appearance. They feed in young flower buds inducing discoloration and other symptoms which resemble frost damage. Measures applied to control aphids will also control suckers.

CAPSID BUGS feed on buds, leaves and young fruits, causing marked bumps and other malformations of the fruit and tattered holes in the leaves. Malathion, dimethoate or formothion applied immediately before and after flowering will check the damage.

WINTER MOTH caterpillars feed in the opening buds and on young leaves and can cause a lot of damage when they are abundant. Thorough spraying with trichlorphon just as the buds are opening will kill the young caterpillars. Placing grease-bands around the trunks in October, will also trap the wingless female winter moths as they climb up the trees from the soil to lay their eggs. Vegetable greases are used and these may be applied on prepared paper strips. Animal or mineral greases should not be used as they

may cause permanent injury to the tree.

FRUIT TREE RED SPIDER MITES are usually only troublesome where the use of tar-oil washes during the winter or persistent insecticides in the post-blossom period have killed off natural predators and allowed the pest to increase unchecked. Mite eggs overwinter on the trees and hatch from May onwards. Damaging colonies build up on the leaves in early summer causing discoloration which may be followed by severe bronzing and premature leaf-fall.

Spraying thoroughly with malathion, dimethoate or formothion immediately after blossoming may check this pest and the use of dinocap to control powdery mildew also helps to control it. An alternative is to apply a DNOC-petroleum winter-wash in February to kill overwintering mite eggs and this will also control aphids, suckers and capsids. Special care must be taken when using this material, and the manufacturers' instructions should be strictly observed.

Diseases

CANKER, a serious disease of apples, shows as sunken cankers on the shoots, which can cause severe die-back if the branches are girdled. Remove badly affected smaller branches. On the larger branches cut out diseased tissues until left with a clean wound and paint with a proprietary canker paint. In severe cases spray with

Above, left: Apple attacked by codling moth. Above, centre: Apple sawfly damage to fruits. Above: Capsid damage to apples.

bordeaux mixture or liquid copper just before leaf fall, at 50% leaf fall and in spring when the buds start to swell. Canker is often worse on trees in poorly drained soil.

SCAB shows as brown or blackish scabs on the fruit and, in severe cases, the fruit may crack. Small blisters develop on shoots and later become scab-like. Leaves are also affected and show olive green blotches and often fall prematurely. Remove these scabby shoots. Spray with 2½% lime sulphur* at green cluster and pink bud, and 1% lime sulphur** at petal fall and fruitlet stages *or* spray at these times and post-blossom as necessary with captan, *or* apply thiophanate-methyl *or* benomyl starting at bud burst and repeating at 14-day intervals until mid-July, if necessary.
* 'Stirling Castle' and 'St. Cecilia' should not be sprayed with lime sulphur.
** 'Beauty of Bath', 'Belle de Boskoop', 'Blenheim Orange', 'Cox's Orange Pippin', 'Duchess's Favourite', 'Lane's Prince Albert', 'Lord Derby', 'Newton Wonder' and 'Rival' are sometimes sulphur-shy and should not be sprayed post-blossom with lime sulphur. Lime sulphur should not be applied after flowering to those trees not sprayed with it before blossoming.

POWDERY MILDEW. This fungus overwinters in the buds, so that in spring the emerging growth is already diseased and covered with a white powdery coating of spores. Affected blossoms and leaves wither and fall. Remove and burn badly affected shoots. Spray with dinocap at pink bud and, if necessary, repeat at 7 to 14-day intervals until mid-July. Thiophanate-methyl can also be used, starting at green cluster and repeating at 14 day intervals, and benomyl may also give some control. If a DNOC-petroleum winter wash is used to kill over-wintering mite eggs (see p. 76) this will also help to control mildew.

BROWN ROT is caused by a fungus which enters through wounds. Affected fruits should be removed and burned as soon as noticed, whether on the tree, on the ground or in the store, as the disease cannot be controlled very effectively by spraying with a fungicide. There is some evidence, however, that thiophanate-methyl applied in mid-August and again early in September will reduce rotting of apples in store.

BITTER PIT affects only the fruits, producing slightly sunken pits on the surface of the skin and small brown areas of tissue immediately beneath the pits and scattered throughout the flesh. The exact cause is unknown, but it appears to be connected with a shortage of water at critical times. It can be avoided to some extent by mulching well to conserve

Above: Colonies of woolly aphid on apples. Right: Apple canker showing a branch nearly girdled.

moisture and by watering in dry periods.

It also apparently results from conditions within the tree that induce a deficiency of calcium (see p. 11) within the fruits. The incidence of bitter pit can be greatly reduced by applying sprays of hydrated calcium nitrate at strengths ranging from 0.5% to 1% (i.e. 4 to 8 oz. (112 to 224 g.) in 5 gal. (22 l.) water). Spray four times at three-weekly intervals starting in mid-June.

HONEY FUNGUS frequently brings about the sudden death of apple trees. The fungus shows as white fan-shaped sheets of growth beneath the bark of the roots and the trunk of the tree at ground level. Affected plants should be dug out with as many of the roots

Right: A blossom truss infected by mildew. Below: Apple scab.

APPLES

Right: Apples badly infected with brown rot. Right, below: Bitter pit: brown spots showing through the skin and in the flesh.

as possible and the soil should be sterilized with 2% formalin solution, or should be changed completely. A proprietary product containing a phenolic emulsion could also be used.

FIREBLIGHT can affect apple trees (see p. 87).

PEARS

Pears are not quite so easy to grow as apples in this country. They flower earlier in the season than apples and are therefore more susceptible to late spring frosts. Therefore, a warm sheltered position should be selected.

The rootstocks should be carefully selected, since they can influence considerably the behaviour of the cultivar. Rootstocks from the quince range are the most suitable, because they bring trees into bearing at an early age and are ideal for the bush, pyramid and other restricted forms, being moderately vigorous to semi-dwarfing in habit. The quince rootstocks in use today, are Malling Quince A and Malling Quince C. Both are suitable for the general range of trees in the small garden. Trees on Quince C come into cropping slightly earlier and do not make as much growth as on Quince A.

Some cultivars of pears do not make a good union with quince when budded or grafted, and these should be double worked, using a compatible cultivar of pear (such as 'Beurré Hardy') as the intermediate stock. Cultivars requiring double working include 'Bristol Cross', 'Dr Jules Guyot', 'Doyenné d'Été', 'Marguerite Marillat', 'Marie Louise', 'Packham's Triumph', 'Souvenir de Congrès', 'Thompson's' and 'Williams' Bon Chrétien'.

Eleven-year-old 'Doyenné du Comice' on Quince A rootstock. Note abundant flowering.

Eleven-year-old 'Doyenné du Comice' on pear rootstock. Not suited to gardens because of very vigorous growth and late bearing.

Selection of cultivar is another matter which requires careful thought. In practice all pear cultivars can be regarded as self-sterile, that is, they will not set fruit with their own pollen and need pollen from another cultivar before a crop can be obtained. If there is space for only two or three trees, it is essential to choose cultivars which will act as pollinators of one another. See list on p. 120.

Pruning

Pears are pruned in much the same way as apples (pp.55–56) and for similar reasons. They can be cut back harder if necessary without the fear of rampant growth being produced, as so often happens with apples. Pears are on the whole more upright in growth than apples and make excellent pyramids.

For the formation of young trees in the various forms grown, the winter pruning is on similar lines to that of apples.

Nearly all pears are similar in growth – though some are stronger than others – bearing fruit on short spurs on two-year and older wood. Two popular exceptions, which are tip-bearers and therefore should be treated accordingly, are 'Joséphine de Malines' and 'Jargonelle' (see p. 61). The laterals of most other cultivars should be pruned back to three or four buds. Shorten the leaders by about a third of their length, or according to where growth is required.

As the trees get older it may be necessary to remove branches here and there to let in light and air, and replacement leaders may be formed from laterals. Spur systems will require pruning and thinning from time to time for the continued production of good quality fruit.

The details of the summer

Pears grown as dwarf pyramids; spacing is 4 to 5 ft (1.2–1.5 m.) between the plants by 7 ft (2 m.) between the rows.

pruning of pears are the same as those described for apples on p. 62, but starting in early July. *Do not summer prune any tree which is not making satisfactory growth.*

Yields

These are generally lower than with apples and possibly vary more from year to year. A well-grown cordon in full bearing will in favourable conditions yield 12 lb. (5.5 kg.) or more of fruit, but the amateur may have to be satisfied with an average of 3 to 5 lbs. (1.5 to 2.5 kg.). The corresponding figures for dwarf pyramids are 15 lb. (7 kg.) or more with an average of 5 to 6 lb. (2.5 kg.), a bush tree on quince 100 to 120 lb. (45 to 55 kg.) or more with an average of 40 to 50 lb. (18 to 23 kg.). The yield of an espalier will largely depend on the size of the tree, but it cannot be expected to give

much more than half that of a bush tree on similar stock, probably less.

Bush Tree

This is the most easily managed form of tree.

ROOTSTOCKS AND SPACING
Quince C (moderately dwarfing). Suitable for strong soils, strong-growing cultivars. Not suitable where conditions are poor. Plant at 10 to 14 feet (3 to 4.3 m.) apart.
Quince A (semi-vigorous). Best all-round stock. If in doubt Quince A should be used. Plant at 12 to 15 feet (3.5 to 4.5 m.) apart.

PRUNING
The pruning of bush pears is much the same as bush apples. During early years pears are best pruned somewhat lightly. Once they have started cropping they will tolerate more severe pruning than apples, both as regards leader tipping and the shortening of

lateral shoots. Pears make spurs more readily than apples, and as the tree grows older these are apt to become too numerous and should be thinned out from time to time (p. 86), otherwise the fruit will tend to be of poor size and quality.

Cordon

ROOTSTOCKS AND SPACING
Quince C (moderately dwarfing) or Quince A (semi-vigorous). Plant at 2½ to 3 feet (60 to 90 cm.) apart in the rows. Rows not less than 6 feet (1.8 m.) apart. Plant as for cordon apples (p. 66) For support systems see apples (p. 65).

PRUNING AND TRAINING
As for cordon apples (p. 67), except that the summer pruning of pears can be started about a week earlier.

Dwarf Pyramid

ROOTSTOCKS AND SPACING
Quince A or Quince C. Plant at 4 to 5 feet (1.2 to 1.5 m.) apart in the

Pruning Dwarf Pyramids

A. *Two-year-old pear before winter pruning.*

B. *After pruning. The leader has been cut back to about 10 in. (25.5 cm.) and the laterals to 8 in. (20 cm.).*

C. *The same tree before summer pruning in July. All branch leaders are cut to 5 or 6 leaves above the basal cluster. Shoots arising directly from the branches are cut to 3 buds and those arising from laterals or spurs to 1 leaf beyond the basal cluster.*

D. *The same tree in the following winter after the central leader has been cut back to 10 in. (25.5 cm.). The branch leaders are not pruned in winter, but any secondary growth after the previous summer pruning is cut back to one bud.*

E. *The same tree in the following July before pruning.*

F. *After summer pruning. All branch leaders, but not the central leader have been cut back to 5 or 6 leaves.*

G. *Five-year-old pyramid pear in winter.*

rows and preferably with 7 feet (2 m.) between the rows.

PLANTING

Maidens are best. For general directions see p. 54.

PRUNING

Maiden Tree: Immediately the buds start to grow in the spring cut back to height of about 20 in. (50 cm.). Shorten any side shoots over 6 in. (15 cm.) long to five good buds.

In the following winter, shorten the leader to leave some 8 to 10 in. (20 to 25 cm.) of new growth, cutting to a bud pointing in the opposite direction to that of the bud chosen the previous spring, this helps to keep the leader straight. Cut back laterals to 6 to 8 in. (15 to 20 cm.) to a downward or outward pointing bud.

In subsequent summers (July in southern England, but later further north) cut mature branch leaders (but not the central leader) to 5 or 6 leaves beyond the basal

E

F

cluster of leaves. Laterals arising directly from the branches are cut back to three leaves and those arising from existing laterals or spurs to one leaf beyond the basal cluster. In mid-August or early September shorten in the same manner any that were not mature in July and have since become longer.

In subsequent winters, shorten the central leader to leave 8 to 10 in. (20 to 25 cm.) of new growth, cutting to a bud pointing in the opposite direction to that of the bud to which the shoot was pruned the previous winter. Cut back to one good bud beyond the point of origin any secondary growth that may have resulted from the summer pruning.

When the trees have reached a height of about 7 feet (2 m.) it is best to restrict their growth. This can be done by cutting back the central leader by a half in May and not in the winter. In subsequent years they should be cut to ½ in. (12.7 mm.) in May. Any

other shoots that need restriction, such as those arising from the top of the tree or branch leaders growing into adjacent trees, can be treated in the same way.

Any thinning out of branches or spurs is best done in winter. N.B. During first few years remove any blossom that may have formed on the central leader, as side branches, not fruits, are required here.

Espalier
ROOTSTOCKS AND SPACING
Quince C (moderately dwarfing). Only suitable where a very small tree of 2 or 3 tiers is required and conditions for growth are good. Plant at 12 to 15 feet (3.5 to 4.5 m.). Quince A (semi-vigorous). Normally the best to use. Plant at 15 to 20 feet apart (4.5 to 6 m.).

SUPPORT SYSTEM AND PLANTING
Horizontal wires should be stretched at intervals of 1 foot (30 cm.) between posts, or between

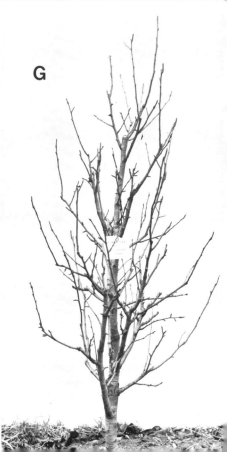

G

straining eyes on walls or fences up to the desired height. Maidens can be planted and trained, or partly trained trees can be bought.

PRUNING AND TRAINING

In the first winter after planting a maiden tree cut back to a good bud about 2 in. (5 cm.) above the first wire. Make this cut as near as possible to a point where there are two good buds fairly close below it (not necessarily next to one another) one bud facing to the right and the other to the left. It is the growth produced from these two buds which will form the first tier. When growth starts rub out any buds between these three.

In the first summer, train the shoot arising from the top bud vertically upwards, tying it to a cane fastened to the wire for the purpose. Train the shoots from the two lower buds to canes at an angle of 45°. If one grows faster than the other raise the weaker one to a more vertical position. At

Pruning Espaliers
Above, left: A maiden pear tree cut back to 2 in. (5 cm.) above the bottom wire. Above: Growth in the next summer. Below: In the following and succeeding summers the leading upright shoot is cut back to 2 in. (5 cm.) above the wire support. Right, above: The same 3-tier espalier in summer. Right, below: This tree has been extended to 5 tiers and will have further tiers added by cutting back the leading upright shoot.

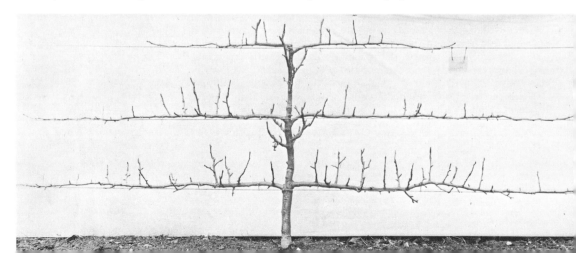

the end of the season lower the canes and shoots and tie them to the first wire. Prune back to 4 to 5 in. (10 to 13 cm.) any other shoots arising from the central stem.

In the second and subsequent winters, the process as described in the first winter is repeated until the top wire is reached and then only two shoots are allowed to grow from the vertical leader. Train these in opposite directions along the top wire.

The leading shoot of each tier is left unpruned unless growth has been poor and the stimulus of winter pruning is necessary. In such instances tip the previous summer's growth by a quarter to a third, pruning to a bud facing in the required direction.

Once a tier has reached the required length prune back the leader to $\frac{1}{2}$ in. (1 cm.) each May.

In second and subsequent summers, starting in early July, the three new shoots arising from the vertical stem are treated in the same way as those in the first year.

The leading shoots from existing tiers are also tied being careful not to tie them down to the horizontal too early as this can depress their growth.

Laterals (side-shoots) of current season's growth arising directly from the tiers or from previously pruned laterals or spurs are summer pruned by the Modified Lorette System see p. 67. Spurs arising from the central stem are also pruned in the same way.

Spur systems on long established espaliers which have become too long or complicated should be shortened or simplified in the winter and the subsequent growth pruned in the summer as described in the preceding paragraph.

Grassing down

Growing pears in grass is not usual, unless some check in growth is needed for cordons or dwarf pyramid trees.

Manuring

For general principles see p. 9. Pears need more nitrogen than apples and can often with advantage be given annual light dressings of farmyard manure or compost.

The following dressings or their equivalents will generally be found suitable for established trees growing normally on a medium soil in reasonably good heart.

Annual dressings in February of 1 to 1½ oz. (33 to 50 g.) of sulphate of ammonia and ½ to ¾ oz. (17 to 25 g.) of sulphate of potash to the square yard (sq. m.). Superphosphate 1½ to 2 oz. (50 to 66 g.) to the square yard (sq. m.) applied every two or three years. If farmyard manure or compost is given then ½ oz. (17 g.) of sulphate of potash should be ample. Where trees are in grass an extra ½ to ¾ oz. (17 to 25 g.) of sulphate of ammonia may be necessary a month after the first application.

Fruit thinning

For general principles see p. 71. Pears as a rule need less thinning than apples, but the time to do it is when the fruitlets start to turn downwards.

Most cultivars, if they are carrying a good crop, and well-sized fruits are to be obtained, need thinning to singles or at most two fruits per cluster.

Picking

For general principles see p. 72. Time of picking is of great importance with pears. Ripening varies with season and locality and it is not possible to give definite dates for picking. The best test of readiness is to lift the fruit slightly and then twist it gently. If it parts easily from the tree, it is ready to come. Early cultivars (e.g. 'Williams' Bon Chrétien') should not remain too long on the tree; they should be picked whilst still green and hard. It is better to pick them a little early than too late; if picked too late they will ripen unevenly, and usually go 'sleepy' in the centre while the outside remains comparatively hard.

Later cultivars must not be picked too early or they will tend to shrivel and fail to develop their full flavour. Leave very late cultivars (e.g. 'Catillac', 'Black Worcester', 'Olivier des Serres') as long as possible on the tree.

Storing

The same general principles apply (see p. 74) except that pears will keep longer under lower temperatures than those quoted for apples: ideally between 32° to 34°F (0° to 1°C.) though this is seldom possible for amateurs. The temperature should not fall below freezing point.

The fruits are not wrapped but are best laid out singly on shelves or trays where they can be frequently and easily inspected. This is especially important as they ripen, for most pears remain at their best for only a very short period.

Pears undergo only a slight change in skin colour from green to yellow-green during normal storage and they do not always soften appreciably in these conditions. They can be ripened and conditioned properly by bringing them, at the correct time, into a warm room a few days before required.

Recommended cultivars

Jargonelle, *Aug*
Williams' Bon Chrétien★, *Sep*
Gorham, *Sep*
Fondante d'Automne★, *Sep to Oct*
Merton Pride★, *Sep to Oct*
Onward★, *Sep to Oct*
Laxton's Foremost, *Sep to Oct*
Bristol Cross, *Sep to Oct*
Beurré Superfin★, *Oct*
Louise Bonne of Jersey, *Oct*
Beurré Hardy, *Oct*
Comte de Lamy★, *Oct to Nov*
Conference, *Oct to Nov*
Emile d'Heyst, *Oct to Nov*
Seckle★, *Oct to Nov*
Marie Louise★, *Oct to Nov*
Thompson's★, *Oct to Nov*
Doyenné du Comice★, *Nov*
Beurré Dumont★, *Nov to Dec*
Packham's Triumph, *Nov to Dec*
Winter Nelis★, *Nov to Jan*
Joséphine de Malines★, *Dec to Jan*
Easter Beurré, *Mar to Apr*

FREEZING
'Williams' and 'Comice' retain texture better than some other cultivars.

POLLINATION
'Seckle' and 'Williams' will not pollinate each other. 'Bristol Cross' is not suitable as a pollinator.

Pests

BIRDS especially tits, will peck ripening pears. Protect them with netting or enclose individual fruits in paper bags or collars.

APHIDS infest young growth and distort the leaves. Spray with tar oil in December or January to kill overwintering eggs or with malathion, dimethoate or formothion just before blossoming to kill young aphids.

★ Good flavour.

PEAR LEAF BLISTER MITES produce characteristic brown pustules in the leaves. Severe infestations may cause premature leaf-fall but most do little permanent harm. On a small scale, hand-pick and destroy infested leaves in the summer. Otherwise apply lime-sulphur at the end of March.

PEAR MIDGE is a localised pest which may attack the same tree year after year. Small maggots feed in the young fruitlets which are distorted and discoloured and drop prematurely. Collection and destruction of infested fruitlets will reduce the numbers of maggots carried over from one season to the next. Spray with BHC or fenitrothion at the early white bud stage.

Diseases

SCAB shows on the fruit as blackish scabs and in severe cases cracking occurs. On leaves it produces olive-green blotches, and affected shoots become blistered and scabby. Diseased shoots should be cut out and burned. Spray with captan or benomyl or thiophanate-methyl at bud burst, green cluster, white bud, petal fall and as necessary post-blossom.

FIREBLIGHT causes the flowers to become blackened and shrivelled. It then spreads down the shoots causing them to die back but the leaves on affected shoots, although brown and withered, do not fall. Fireblight is a notifiable disease and when it is suspected that a tree has been attacked the

Above: Pears and apples can be protected from birds by enclosing each fruit in a paper, polythene or muslin bag.

Left: Pear scab.

owner is obliged to notify the local representative of the Ministry of Agriculture, Fisheries and Food. Full instructions will then be given as to how the tree should be treated.

CANKER can affect pears, especially the cultivar 'Fertility'.

For symptoms and control see p. 76.

BROWN ROT is frequently troublesome on pears. For symptoms and control see p. 77.

HONEY FUNGUS often causes the sudden death of pear trees. For symptoms and control see p. 77.

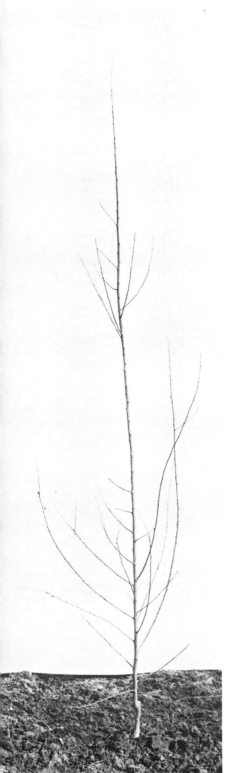

Plums include gages, bullaces and damsons. They will succeed in nearly all kinds of soils, but since they are early-flowering, they do not fruit well in low-lying areas subject to spring frosts. They do not do well either on badly drained cold ground or on very acid soils. These acid soils may, however, be treated by adding lime or old mortar rubble in moderate quantities. Plums require plenty of light and moisture and should not be planted close to large trees, especially those such as elms, which are surface rooting.

In most situations the finest flavour is obtained from plums and gages grown against a warm wall, but very good results can be obtained in the open. They are not very suitable for growing in restricted form, consequently plenty of space should be left at planting.

Manuring

Plums need a liberal amount of nitrogen and are generally grown on cultivated soil. They respond well to bulky organic manures and benefit from moderate dressings

Left: A newly-planted maiden plum tree before staking and pruning.

Right: The same tree staked with two upright stakes and a crosspiece. This method is especially suitable for trees with a long stem. For half-standards the main stem is cut back to 4½ ft (1.4 m.). The side-shoots ('feathers') have been shortened, but are left for a few years to help the thickening of the stem.

of farmyard manure or compost from time to time.

The following are examples of dressings or their equivalents which will generally be found to be suitable for established trees growing normally on moderate to good ground.

(a) Where farmyard manure or compost is readily available an annual light dressing of either, supplemented by $\frac{1}{2}$ to $\frac{3}{4}$ oz. (17 to 25 g.) of sulphate of ammonia and $\frac{1}{2}$ oz. (17 g.) sulphate of potash to the square yard (sq. m.). Superphosphate $1\frac{1}{2}$ to 2 oz. (50 to 66 g.) to the square yard (sq. m.) every two to three years.

(b) $1\frac{1}{2}$ to 2 oz. (50 to 66 g.) sulphate of ammonia and $\frac{1}{2}$ oz. (17 g.) of sulphate of potash to the square yard (sq. m.). Superphosphate $1\frac{1}{2}$ to 2 oz. (50 to 66 g.) to the square yard (sq. m.) every two or three years. Every three years or so, or if the trees are not making satisfactory growth, give a light dressing of farmyard manure or compost in addition.

Support (see also p. 72).
Heavily-laden branches must be adequately supported or breakage will occur, with the subsequent risk of infection by silver leaf.

Yields
Many plums are self-sterile and will therefore not produce a crop unless the flowers receive pollen from another cultivar. For details see lists of recommended cultivars and pollination tables (pp. 120–121).

Yields vary considerably from year to year and also according to weather, cultivar, soil and treatment, so the following figures should be regarded as only a rough guide. They show, however, the potential value of a few well-grown plum trees in the garden.

Half-standards, bush and pyramid trees of the heavier cropping cultivars such as 'Victoria' on St Julien A will yield little or nothing for 5 or 6 years. For the next 10 years well-grown standard or bush trees may average 40 to 50

lb. (18 to 23 kg.), with 150 lb. (68 kg.) or more in a good year. When they reach full bearing they may average 100 to 120 lb. (45 to 52 kg.), with a maximum of about 180 lb. (81 kg.). Trees on the more vigorous Myrobalan and Brompton will give somewhat higher yields. Pyramids yield less.

The shy-cropping cultivars, which include most gages, may only give half these yields or less and be more variable in cropping.

The yield from the fan-trained

Ten-year-old plum ('Pershore') on Myrobalan B, a widely compatible rootstock, but often too vigorous for gardens.

tree will depend on its size, with an average of about 15 to 25 lb. (7 to 11 kg.) for a full-grown tree.

Half-Standard and Bush Trees
ROOTSTOCKS
Some plum cultivars are incompatible with certain rootstocks

Ten-year-old half-standard plum ('Pershore') on Common Plum, a rootstock more suitable for gardens. For cultivars incompatible with Common Plum, St Julien A will produce trees of this size.

e.g. 'President' on Common Plum. The most suitable rootstock for the small garden is St Julien A (semi-dwarfing). It is very satisfactory for all forms of tree and is compatible with all cultivars. Pixie is a new rootstock, more dwarfing than St Julien A, but not yet freely available.

Brompton (vigorous) makes an excellent stock for all cultivars, but is rather too vigorous for the small garden. It is less suitable for bush trees or pyramids. Myrobalan B (vigorous) makes a large tree, and is excellent for all cultivars except a few such as 'Oullins Golden Gage' and 'Count Althann's' because of incompatibility.

On St Julien A, plant at 12 to 15 feet (3.5 to 4.5 m.) apart. On Brompton or Myrobalan B, plant at 18 to 20 feet (5.5 to 6 m.)

PLANTING

Maidens are to be preferred, since they can be trained as desired, but suitably trained two- and three-year trees are satisfactory. Trees should be staked on planting.

PRUNING

Owing to the risk of silver leaf infection during autumn and winter, pruning should either be carried out in the spring, when growth has started, in order that wounds may heal quickly, or immediately after fruiting in the summer or early autumn. Large cuts should be pared and covered with bitumen paint or soft grafting wax. It is not wise to remove big branches during the winter.

In the first year, maiden trees are cut back in spring after planting – just before growth begins – to about 4½ feet (1.3 m.) for half-standard and 3 feet (90 cm.) for a bush, 6 to 8 in. (15 to 20 cm.) above the point at which it is desired the lowest branches should originate. Space the branches so that they are about 3 in. (7.5 cm.) apart. Shoots lower on the stem should not be removed at once as they help thicken the stem; they should be left for 2 or 3 years, being shortened back to 4 or 5 leaves during the summer.

Two- and three-year-old trees are best left unpruned for a year.

In the second year, choose 3 or 4 shoots of the previous season's growth, of uniform vigour and as evenly spaced round the tree as possible, and cut these back by about half in the spring. Cut out the remainder, particularly those forming narrow V-angles which may be liable to break under the weight of a heavy crop.

In the third year, the leading shoots of spreading cultivars like 'Victoria' may need shortening back for another year or two. Otherwise all that is usually necessary is to cut out dead, broken, rubbing and crossing

Far left: Two-year-old half-standard tree before pruning, which is done just before growth starts in the spring.

Left: The same tree after pruning. The shoots that are to form the main branches are cut back by half.

branches and not to allow the head of the tree to become over-crowded. This work should only be done in the growing season between June and August when the risk of silver leaf infection is at its lowest.

Pyramid

Pyramid plums have not been tried very extensively but, with careful pruning a moderate sized, compact tree can be produced which is very suitable for the garden.

ROOTSTOCKS
St Julien A (semi-dwarfing) is the most suitable rootstock, planted at 10–12 feet (3–3.5 m.) apart.

PLANTING
Plant as maidens, preferably in the autumn (for general directions see p. 54).

PRUNING AND TRAINING
The main leader of the maiden tree should be cut back in April to about 5 feet (1.5 m.) above ground level and the feathers (side branches) cut by half, except those within 18 in. (46 cm.) of the ground which are removed.

In the first summer, prune in the third week of July when the young shoots have finished growing. Shorten the branch leaders to 8 in. (20 cm.) to a downward facing bud, and prune laterals to 6 in. (15 cm.). Do not prune the central leader.

In subsequent years, shorten

Far left: Four-year-old tree before pruning.

Left: The same tree after pruning. The branch leaders have been shortened by about half.

the central leader by two-thirds each April. When the tree has reached 9 feet (2.7 m.) in height, the central leader should be cut back hard to about one inch (2.5 cm.) every May, to keep the tree at that height.

Every summer, during the third week of July, shorten branch leaders to 8 in. (20 cm.) and cut laterals to 6 in. (15 cm.), preferably to downward facing buds.

Any shoot near the top which grows up and competes with the main leader should be removed.

Fan-trained
To cover a wall space with plums, the most suitable form of tree is the fan. Such trees produce the finest-flavoured gages.

ROOTSTOCKS
St Julien A (semi-dwarfing) is probably the most satisfactory rootstock, planted at 15 to 18 feet (4.5 to 5.5 m.).

Eight-year-old 'Victoria' grown in the pyramid form.

PLANTING
Maidens can be planted, or if preferred partially trained trees can be bought from the nurseryman. The tree should be planted at 6 to 9 in. (15 to 23 cm.) from the wall, with the stem sloping slightly towards it.

The support system consists of wires spaced about 6 in. (15 cm.) or two brick courses apart horizontally.

For other general directions see p. 54.

PRUNING AND TRAINING
The framework can be built up on the same lines as the peach (p. 97). Thereafter the treatment is somewhat different as plums fruit on both old and new wood. Shoots can be trained on to extend the existing framework as with the peach. Likewise, new shoots can be trained as necessary to fill empty spaces or replace worn-out shoots. Remove shoots growing directly towards or away from the wall quite early in the season when new growth is starting. Pinch out the tips of other laterals not required for extension or replacement, when they have made 6 or 7 leaves. Fruiting laterals can be left closer than with the peach.

After the crop has been picked, remove dead wood, shorten shoots that have already been pinched back by about half, and do any necessary tying in.

Strong vertical shoots must be cut out or tied down towards the horizontal.

Manuring
Though plums usually do best when given plenty of nitrogen, care must be taken not to overdo this, particularly in the case of wall trees, or over-vigorous growth will result. A light mulch of farmyard manure in April, following application of $\frac{1}{2}-\frac{3}{4}$ oz. (17 to 25 g.) of sulphate of ammonia or its equivalent to the square yard (sq.

m.) plus $\frac{1}{2}$ oz. (17 g.) of sulphate of potash, will usually be adequate. A dressing of superphosphate, $1\frac{1}{2}$ to 2 oz. (50 to 66 g.) to the square yard (sq. m.) every second or third year, will also be beneficial.

Cultivation

Disturbing the soil encourages suckering, therefore keep cultivation to a minimum. If suckers do occur it is better to pull them up rather than cut them. If neglected they may become troublesome. For root pruning, watering and frost protection see peaches p. 101.

Fruit thinning

For general principles see p. 71.

When a plum tree is carrying a heavy crop, thinning is essential to avoid small, poorly-coloured and flavourless fruit and broken branches. In such cases thin to leave the fruits 2 to 3 in. (5 to 7.5 cm.) or more apart, according to cultivar. It is often best to carry out the process of thinning in two stages; first early in June, and again later to allow for any dropping of fruits during the stone-hardening period. At the time, beginners often think such thinning too drastic, but when the fruit has swollen it is often seen that too little thinning has been done.

Picking

The time to pick the fruit depends to some extent on its use. The best flavour is obtained by allowing it to remain on the tree until fully ripe, but if required for jam, bottling or cooking, plums are generally best picked slightly under-ripe.

Trees of dessert plums should be gone over several times, the individual fruits being picked as they reach the required stage of maturity. Cooking plums are also

Right, above: A fan-trained plum in its first summer: two good and balanced side-shoots have been trained from the central stem.

Right: The same tree in mid-July, when the central shoot is cut out.

A mature fan-trained plum.

Choice of cultivars

Gages are the most desirable of the plums because of their flavour, but many are all too prone to split and become infected with brown rot when the weather is wet. Consequently they should not be planted in rainy localities. They are likely to do best in warm sunny conditions in areas of low rainfall.

A considerable number of plums, of which 'Victoria' is one, will set a full crop with their own pollen, but others will not unless pollinated by another cultivar. It is necessary to make sure within which category the cultivar falls and plan accordingly (see pp. 120–121). Recommended cultivars which are self-fertile have been marked thus: (*s.f.*).

It is wise to plant a regular bearing, prolific-blossoming plum with those cultivars that require cross-pollination, and the following are specially suitable: for

best picked over two or three times and not cleared at one picking.

Gages and those plums liable to split in wet weather may have to be picked before they are ripe, so sacrificing some flavour, but avoiding some splitting.

Plums intended for keeping need special care in handling and must be picked dry and with the stalk; otherwise they may develop brown rot.

Storing

Plums are best eaten straight from the tree, though it is possible to keep them for two or three weeks more by picking them slightly under-ripe, placing each fruit in wrapping paper and storing them carefully. In the ordinary way, however, plums will not keep for more than a few days after picking.

Left: A heavily-laden branch in early June before thinning.

Right: After the first thinning.

early blossoming, 'Denniston's Superb', and for the late ones, 'Oullins Golden Gage'. 'Victoria' flowers in mid-season but is a valuable pollinator for both early and late blossoming sorts.

Recommended cultivars (see also p. 121).

DESSERT

Early Laxton, *late July to early Aug*

Oullins Golden Gage, *(s.f.) mid-Aug*

Count Althann's Gage, *mid to late Aug*

Early Transparent Gage★, *(s.f.) mid to late Aug*

Goldfinch, *mid to late Aug*

Denniston's Superb *(s.f.)*, *late Aug*

Victoria, *(s.f.) late Aug to early Sep*

Cambridge Gage★, *late Aug to early Sep*

Old Green Gage★, *late Aug to early Sep*

Jefferson★, *late Aug to early Sep*

Kirke's★, *late Aug to early Sep*

Merton Gem★, *early to mid-Sep*

Edwards, *early to mid-Sep*

Golden Transparent★, *(s.f.) early to mid-Sep*

Laxton's Delight, *Sep*

Severn Cross, *(s.f.) mid to late Sep*

Ariel, *mid to late Sep*

Coe's Golden Drop, *late Sep*

CULINARY

Early Rivers (Early Prolific), *late July to early Aug*

Czar, *(s.f.) early Aug*

Black Prince, *early to mid Aug*

Pershore (Yellow Egg), *(s.f.) mid-Aug*

Purple Pershore, *(s.f.) mid to late Aug*

Victoria, *(s.f.) late Aug to Sep*

Warwickshire Drooper, *(s.f.) early to mid-Sep*

Marjorie's Seedling, *(s.f.) late Sep to early Oct*

PROMISING CULTIVAR

Anna Späth, *late Sep to early Oct*

★ Good flavour.
(s.f.) = self-fertile; a single tree can be planted.

RECOMMENDED DAMSON CULTIVARS (all *s.f.*)

Merryweather, *early Sep*

Bradley's, *mid-Sep*

Farleigh Damson, *mid-Sep*

Prune (Shropshire Damson), *Sep to Oct*

Pests

APHIDS infest young shoots and also colonise the undersides of older leaves. Spray with tar oil in December or January to kill overwintering eggs; or with malathion, dimethoate, or formothion in the pre-blossom period to kill young aphids.

BIRDS. Bullfinches are responsible for considerable damage to over-wintering fruit buds, often resulting in total loss of crop. Preventive measures should therefore be taken where possible either by netting or cottoning.

Right: Mealy plum aphids.

Below: Plum shoots showing damage by plum leaf curling aphid.

Diseases

SILVER LEAF can cause progressive die back of a tree, and a purplish-brown stain is produced in the inner tissues. Leaves show an unhealthy silvery discoloration. All diseased branches must then be cut out to 4 to 6 inches (10 to 15 cm.) behind the point where the stain ceases. Seal all wounds with a good protective paint.

FALSE SILVER LEAF is a physiological disorder which is probably more common than true silver leaf. The foliage shows a silvery discoloration but most of the leaves on a tree are affected at the same time, and there is little or no die-back. No stain is apparent in the branch bearing silvered leaves. Malnutrition and an irregular supply of moisture in the soil can cause this trouble, so affected trees should be mulched, watered and fed as necessary.

BROWN ROT (see p. 77) can cause serious losses of fruit, if diseased plums are not removed and destroyed.

BACTERIAL CANKER shows along the branches as elongated flattened cankers which exude copious gum. The buds of an affected branch do not burst, or if leaves do develop they are small and yellow and eventually die. On the leaves of other branches small

Silver leaf of plum. Top healthy leaves, below silvery leaves produced by a diseased branch.

brown spots develop and the discoloured tissues fall away leaving holes. Remove badly cankered branches and dead wood and paint all wounds with a good protective paint. Spray with bordeaux mixture in mid-August, mid-September and mid-October.

FIREBLIGHT. Plums are *not* affected by fireblight.

PEACHES AND NECTARINES

These are treated together, as the nectarine is only a variety of the peach with a smooth skin and a slightly less robust constitution. They are best grown as fan-trained trees on a wall. Excellent results have however been obtained from trees grown as bushes in the open and sometimes in apparently most unlikely situations but only when spring frosts have not been troublesome. Successful crops have been obtained from trees grown from peach stones; in many suburban gardens bushes laden with hundreds of fruits have been reared within a period of eight years with a minimum of care and trouble. Lack of wall space should not therefore deter amateurs with the room to plant peaches as bushes in the open. Good soil drainage is very important for the peach.

Nectarines are not likely to succeed as bushes and should be grown fan-trained on a sunny wall.

Fan trained

The fan is the most reliable way of growing peaches and nectarines in this country, either against a wall or a fence. The object is to cover the wall space with branches radiating out from the tree at a few inches above ground level, like the ribs of a fan, so that each branch receives the maximum amount of sun and air.

A southern aspect is preferable, but one facing west can be satisfactory. A north aspect is not suitable. Time and care are needed to grow this type of tree well.

ROOTSTOCKS

St Julien A (Semi-dwarfing) and Brompton (Vigorous).

Plant at 18 to 24 feet (5.5 to 7.5 m.) apart, though trees can be grown more closely if growth is restricted.

PLANTING

For general directions on planting see p. 54.

It is worth while treating peaches and nectarines with special care, as good results are more likely to be obtained if the site is well prepared. The ground should first be trenched. Where the soil is known to be very acid, a dressing of lime will be necessary. In heavy soils, lime rubble is the best form to use but only in moderate quantities. Peaches and nectarines will not succeed on a soil with a high lime content. Good drainage is essential. To improve drainage on a heavy soil liberal quantities of brick rubble covered with chopped-up turves may be placed in the bottom of the hole. Autumn planting is preferable.

Maidens can be planted, or partly-trained trees can be bought from the nurseryman. The trees are planted 6 to 9 in. (15 to 23 cm.) away from the wall with the stem sloping slightly towards it.

A system of wiring is desirable, the wires being spaced horizontally, at 6 in. (15 cm.), or two brick-courses apart.

PRUNING AND TRAINING

When pruning a peach it must be remembered that the fruit is borne only on wood of the previous year's growth. It is also necessary to be able to distinguish between wood buds (pointed) and fruit buds (plump and round). Fruit buds never produce shoots and it is no good cutting back to one if a shoot is required. It is always safe to cut to triple buds as these consist of two blossom buds and a wood bud.

In the spring after planting, just before growth starts, cut the maiden tree back to about 24 in. (60 cm.) above the ground, if possible to a lateral, otherwise to a good bud with a couple of buds below it. Remove all other laterals, cutting them close to main stem. The maiden can also be left unpruned but disbudded, leaving only two well placed shoots.

In the first summer, of the resultant growths select two good shoots, one on either side, about 9 to 12 in. (23 to 30 cm.) above ground. Rub out all other buds, except those right at the top or on the lateral as the case may be.

When the two side shoots are about 18 in. (45 cm.) long, tie to canes placed at an angle of approximately 45° or a little lower. If one shoot grows more strongly than the other it should be temporarily trained at a somewhat lower angle. The main stem above these two shoots should be carefully cut out at the same time. The wound should be protected with a bitumen tree paint.

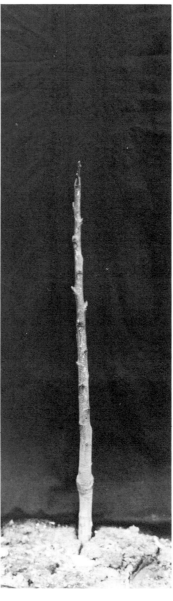

Right, above: In the following summer two of the resulting side shoots at about 9 in. (22 cm.) above the ground are selected and trained along canes at an angle of 45°. All other shoots are removed.

Right, below: When these are about 18 in. (45 cm.) long the main stem is cut out.

for another year, if there is plenty of room and a large tree is wanted cutting back the new branches to 15 in. (38 cm.) or so. Otherwise attention can now be given to fruit production.

In the third summer, allow the end bud on each of the eight branches to grow on and tie them in. Rub out buds growing directly towards or out from the wall. Allow young shoots to grow out from the remaining buds on both the upper and lower sides of the branches, provided these when tied in lie about 4 in. (10 cm.) apart, either rubbing out those not wanted or pinching them back to two or three leaves. These shoots are not normally allowed to grow up much more than 18 in. (45 cm.). If they do, pinch them back unless they are required to extend the framework. Tie them in towards the end of the summer. It is on these shoots that fruit will be produced the following year.

The main treatments, in the fourth and following summers, are deshooting, pinching back and tying in. Deshooting is the removal of superfluous young shoots which, if allowed to grow, would compete with the fruiting wood.

As soon as growth starts in spring, remove shoots growing directly towards or out from the wall. Next deal with the young shoots of the previous year's growth, which should be carrying blossom and wood buds. At the base of these shoots there will nearly always be found two or more wood buds; allow one or two of these to grow out, to form the 'replacement shoot' which will later replace the existing shoot. Allow the terminal bud to grow

Above: A maiden tree after planting.

Above, right: The same tree cut to 24 in. (60 cm.) above the ground.

In February, in the second winter, cut back the two side branches to a bud 12 to 18 in. (30 to 45 cm.) from the main stem.

In the second summer, allow the shoot from the end bud of each branch to grow on and tie it in. Also allow two suitably spaced shoots to grow on the upper side

of each branch and one on the lower side. These, too, must be tied in to the wire, or suitably placed canes, as they grow. Rub out all other buds.

In February, in the third winter, cut back each of the eight branches to a triple bud (upward pointing if possible) so as to leave some 24 to 30 in. (60 to 75 cm.) of ripened wood, of the previous summer's growth.

The previous summer and winter treatments can be repeated

out, but when it has produced about 6 leaves pinch it back to 4 leaves; but if there is plenty of room, it can be left longer and used to extend the existing shoot.

Pinch back to 2 good leaves those shoots growing out where fruits are being allowed to remain, and secondaries arising from these to one leaf. Where there are no fruits, or where they have been removed, pinch out the growing tip when it is no more than an inch (2.5 cm.) long. Where growing tips are crowded they may be entirely removed.

Spread out the operation of deshooting and pinching back over about a fortnight, and start at

Left, above: In the following February both shoots are cut back to a bud at 24 to 30 in. (60 to 75 cm.) from the main stem.
Left, below: The same tree showing good growth of side shoots in the following summer.
Below: The three-year-old tree before winter pruning.

the top of the tree.

Treat shoots to be used to extend the existing framework as described for the third summer.

After the fruit has been picked, if there is wall space to be filled, train on some of the shoots that have just fruited. Any shoots not wanted are cut out, and the replacement shoots tied in in their place. At the same time cut out any dead or diseased wood.

MANURING

Peaches in fertile soil will not require much extra manuring until they start cropping, or growth slows down. Too much nitrogen is likely to encourage over-vigorous growth at the expense of fruiting. A light mulch of farmyard manure applied in May will help to keep the soil moist in the summer.

CULTIVATION

Unless there is adequate wall or fence space it is often difficult to keep fan-shaped trees within bounds, and root pruning may be

needed from time to time (pp. 112–113).

The trees should not be allowed to get dry at the roots. Mulching in the spring and watering in dry spells will help.

Some protection against spring frosts can be obtained by hanging hessian in front of the trees on nights when frost is forecast.

In the north, unless the situation is exceptionally warm and sunny, it is best to rely mainly on early ripening cultivars.

THINNING

To get good-sized peaches on a healthy tree the fruits should be spaced to give one peach to every 9 in. (23 cm.) of wood. Thinning is done in two operations, the first when the fruit is the size of a hazel nut, usually in June. At this stage reduce to singles, spaced at about 4 in. (10 cm.) apart, removing all fruit next to the wall and in places where there is no room for it to swell, but leaving about twice as many fruits as are

Left, above: Three-year-old tree after pruning in February. The new branches have been cut back to about 15 in. (40 cm.).

Left, below: A well-trained established fan peach.

Right, above: Before deshooting a fan-trained peach. The buds on young shoots must be thinned to leave one to grow every 4 in. (10 cm.) or so on both upper and lower sides. One bud should be left at the base to give a replacement shoot. The terminal bud on shoots bearing flowers is allowed to grow on until it has produced about 6 leaves, when it is pinched back to 4 leaves.

Right, below: Deshooting is almost completed.

finally required. When the fruit is about the size of a walnut thin to about 9 inches apart (23 cm.) at the end of June.

PICKING

Peaches must be handled with extreme care. The test for picking is to hold the fruit lightly in the palm of the hand and press it gently at the base near the stalk with the tips of the fingers. If the flesh gives it is ready to pick and will usually come away easily from the tree without pulling. Shallow boxes or chips lined with cotton wool or similar soft material make good receptacles. Keep the peaches in a cool place until they are to be eaten.

Bush Trees

ROOTSTOCKS

St Julien A (Semi-dwarfing).
Plant at 15 to 18 feet (4.5 to 5.5 m.) apart.
Brompton (Vigorous).
Plant at 18 to 24 feet (5.5 to 7.5 m.) apart.

PLANTING

As for fan-shaped tree. A maiden tree is most suitable. 'Rochester' is the best cultivar for growing as a bush.

PRUNING

The maiden is pruned after planting in late April or May, when

buds have started to grow out. Cut back the leader to about 2 feet (60 cm.). Unwanted side shoots are removed entirely, and any that have died are cut back to a strong bud.

Subsequently remove crowding and crossing branches and cut back to a good bud any branch dying back at its tip.

Later, when cropping has pulled down the lower branches, these are cut out altogether. The aim should always be to encourage the growth of strong new wood from the centre of the tree to replace the older branches as they become unfruitful.

MANURING
Generous manuring, as advocated for plums (see p. 92), will probably be needed to induce vigorous growth of new wood, but too much vegetative growth will reduce cropping.

THINNING
In the first year all flowers are removed, and very few fruits should be allowed to mature in the second year. In subsequent years the fruit should be thinned as described on p. 101.

Recommended cultivars: peaches

Duke of York, *mid-July*
Hale's Early, *mid to end July*
Peregrine*, *early Aug*
Rochester, *early Aug*
Royal George*, *late Aug*
Noblesse*, *Aug to Sep*
Bellegarde*, *early to mid-Sep*
Dymond*, *mid to late Sep*

FREEZING
'Hale's Early' is good for freezing.

Recommended cultivars: nectarines

Early Rivers, *mid-July*
John Rivers*, *mid-July*
Lord Napier*, *early Aug*
Humboldt*, *mid-Aug*
Elruge*, *late Aug*
Pine Apple*, *early Sep*

* Good flavour.

Peach with two leaves badly infected with leaf curl.

Pests

APHIDS infest young shoots in the spring and are best controlled by spraying tar-oil in December, to kill overwintering eggs, or malathion, dimethoate or formothion applied after blossoming.

GLASSHOUSE RED SPIDER MITES may be troublesome on plants growing on warm walls. Infested leaves first develop a very fine light mottling on the upper surfaces and later bronze and die. Thorough spraying with malathion may control this pest but it is difficult to check when conditions favour it. Biological control with the predatory mite *Phytoseiulus* should be considered where chemical control fails.

Diseases

PEACH LEAF CURL shows on the leaves as large blisters which are first red but later swell up and turn white. Affected leaves fall early in the season. Spray with bordeaux mixture, liquid copper or 3% lime sulphur in January or February, repeating 10 to 14 days later, and again in the autumn immediately before leaf fall.

BACTERIAL CANKER and SILVER LEAF (see p. 96) and BROWN ROT and the HONEY FUNGUS (see p. 77) can also affect peaches.

SPLIT STONE shows as a deep crack at the stalk end of affected fruit, and within the stone, which is split into two, the kernel rots. This is often caused by several adverse cultural factors, but can be prevented by applying lime if the soil is very acid, by mulching and watering so that the soil does not dry out, and by hand-pollination of the flowers.

SWEET CHERRIES

Sweet cherries are not suitable for a small garden. No dwarfing stocks are yet available and, in whatever form they are grown they make large trees, which are difficult to pick and almost impossible to protect from birds. Moreover, they take a long time to start cropping and at least two trees of different cultivars must be planted as nearly all sweet cherries are self-sterile. Owing to their vigour

A fan-trained sweet cherry.

sweet cherries are not usually suitable for growing on walls.

However, recently released from the research stations is a semi-vigorous stock called Colt which looks promising for the medium-sized garden and could be useful for wall-trained sweet cherries.

Sweet cherries are usually propagated on the wild cherry generally known as mazzard, gaskin or gean. These are all very vigorous.

For those who have sufficient wall space and wish to try growing them as a fan the following cultural details are given.

ROOTSTOCKS
Colt (Semi-vigorous). Plant at 12 to 15 feet (3.5 to 4.5 m.) as a fan, and at 15 feet (4.5 m.) in the open. Malling 12/1 (Vigorous). Plant at 18 to 24 feet (5.5 to 7.5 m.) as a fan. Allow plenty of room, and plant as for fan-shaped plums (p. 92).

PRUNING AND TRAINING

Owing to the risk of silver leaf infection, pruning should not be done in the winter.

The framework can be built up on much the same lines as the peach (p. 97), the branches being spaced a foot or so apart.

Once the tree has been shaped the leading shoots are not cut back. Even when a shoot reaches the top of the wall it is best not to tip it. Where possible shorten it to a weak lateral. If there is none, bend the shoot over and tie it down. This will weaken it and encourage new shoots to break.

Shoots growing directly towards or out from the wall are removed early in the season. All others, except those that are to be trained or to fill an empty space, should have their growing tips pinched out when they have made five or six leaves.

In early autumn remove dead wood. Shorten shoots that have already been pinched back to three or four buds, and do any necessary tying in.

Strong vertical shoots must be cut out or tied down towards the horizontal to repress further growth.

MANURING

Apply a mulch of well-rotted manure or compost in late spring, together with $\frac{1}{2}$ to $\frac{3}{4}$ oz. (17 to 25 g.) of sulphate of potash or its equivalent to the square yard (sq. m.), supplemented by 2 to 3 oz. (66 to 100 g.) of superphos-

phate every two or three years.

CULTIVATION

If a tree is over-vigorous, root pruning may be necessary (pp. 112–113). Take care that trees against walls do not become dry at the roots; a mulch of well-rotted manure or compost, applied in the spring and watering during dry spells will help to conserve soil moisture.

Netting can be used to protect the fruit against birds.

PICKING

Cherries, unless they start cracking, can be left on the tree until they are fully ripe. Once picked they should be eaten as soon as possible, as they quickly lose condition. They cannot be stored.

POLLINATION

Most sweet cherries will not set fruit with their own pollen, and many will not pollinate one another, so that at least two are needed to get a crop (see p. 123). The following are suggested pairs which will cross pollinate:

'Early Rivers' (early) with 'Bigarreau de Schrecken' (early): 'Governor Wood' (mid season) with 'Bigarreau Napoleon' (late).

The following groups will not pollinate each other: 'Early Rivers' and 'Roundel'; any two out of 'Bigarreau de Schrecken', 'Merton Bigarreau', 'Waterloo', 'Merton Favourite'.

Recommended cultivars (see also p. 123)

Early Rivers*, *mid to late June*
Bigarreau de Schrecken*, *late June*
Waterloo*, *late June to early July*
Roundel*, *early July*
Elton*, *early July*
Kent Bigarreau, *early July*
Merton Crane*, *early to mid-July*
Merton Glory, *mid-July*
Van, *mid to late July*
Merton Bigarreau*, *mid to late July*
Bigarreau Gaucher, *mid to late July*
Bradbourne Black*, *late July*
Merton Favourite*, *late July*
Stella. *The first self-fertile sweet cherry. Late July.*

NEW CULTIVAR OF PROMISE

Lambert Compact. *A more dwarf form of 'Lambert'. Self-infertile.*

Pests

BIRDS, especially starlings, eat ripe fruit and bullfinches feed on the buds during the winter. Protect with netting, if possible.

APHIDS, especially the cherry blackfly, infest young shoots causing distortion and checking growth. Spray tar-oil in December or January to kill overwintering eggs, or malathion, dimethoate or formothion in the pre-blossom period to kill young aphids.

Diseases

BACTERIAL CANKER, SILVER LEAF (see p. 96) and BROWN ROT (see p. 77) can affect sweet cherries.

---

* Good flavour.

ACID CHERRIES

Unlike sweet cherries, acid cherries can be satisfactorily grown in the garden, either as bush or as wall trees. Of these 'Morello' is that most commonly grown. Both the 'Morello' and 'Kentish Red' in general use will set full crops with their own pollen and can be planted alone.

Acid cherries on mazzard rootstocks can be grown as bush trees, or as fan-trained specimens. The Malling selected mazzard F 12/1 is recommended. There is also a promising new, semi-vigorous rootstock, called Colt which is not yet freely available.

Bush Tree

ROOTSTOCK
Colt (semi-vigorous). Plant at 12 to 15 feet (3.5 to 4.5 m.).
Malling F 12/1 (vigorous). Plant at 15 to 18 feet (4.5 to 5.5 m.).

PLANTING
Maidens are generally to be preferred but a 2-year tree is suitable. Stake at planting.

PRUNING
Acid cherries fruit only on the previous year's wood, so pruning is aimed at getting a constant and adequate supply of vigorous new growth.

The framework of the bush tree can be formed in the same way as with plums (p. 90). Once the framework has been formed, which may take 3 or 4 years, a certain number of branches should

Pruning out some of the old wood from an acid cherry.

be cut back each year into two-year-old wood in the case of young trees, and into three- and four-year-old wood with older trees. The head should be kept thinned out, and inward or badly crossing branches cut back to wood buds which are often formed at the base of the previous year's growth.

Pruning is best done in the spring after the buds have broken, as wood buds can then be easily distinguished and there is less risk of silver leaf infection.

MANURING
The manurial requirements of acid cherries are similar to those of plums (p. 92).

CULTIVATION
Acid cherries are best grown in cultivated soil and the weeds kept down during the growing season.

PICKING
In the garden acid cherries, unless they start cracking, can be left on the trees until ripe.

Acid cherries are best cut with scissors as pulling the stalk is apt to tear the bark and increase the risk of brown rot infection.

Fan-shaped Tree

ROOTSTOCK

Colt (semi-vigorous). Plant at 12 to 15 feet (3.5 to 4.5 m.). Malling F 12/1 (vigorous). Plant at 15 to 18 feet (4.5 to 5.5 m.).

PLANTING

Any wall, including a north one, is suitable for 'Morello'. Plant as for fan-trained plums (see p. 92).

PRUNING AND TRAINING

Prune as for peaches (p. 97), but side shoots can be left only 2 to 3 in. (5 to 7.5 cm.) apart. With an established tree cut back a proportion of the older branches each year to encourage new growth. The cut surfaces should be painted with one of the proprietary bitumen tree paints.

CULTIVATION

Trees grown against walls must

Above: A fan-trained 'Morello' being tied in. Right before, left after tying in.

Right: The side shoots can be tied in more closely than peaches, about 2 to 3 in. (5 to 7.5 cm.) apart.

not become dry at the roots. Apply a mulch of well-rotted manure or compost in the spring, and water during dry spells. Netting can be used to protect the fruit against birds.

Recommended cultivar

Morello, *Aug to Sep (Self-fertile).*

Pests and Diseases

SILVER LEAF (see p. 96) and BROWN ROT (see p. 77) can be troublesome on acid cherries.

BULLFINCHES AND APHIDS (see p. 106).

FIGS

Figs must have plenty of sun and warmth and the best way of growing them is against a south-facing wall. They are likely to do best in the south and west of England. A wall tree is generally grown as a fan. In a small garden it is sometimes possible to place a fig in a sunny corner provided by two house walls.

PLANTING

Figs are grown on their own roots, and no rootstocks are available. The rooting area of the tree must be restricted or it will make a lot of soft unfruitful wood. This can be done by making a bed about 3 to 4 feet (1 m.) long, 2 to 3 feet (60 to 90 cm.) wide and about 3 feet (90 cm.) deep, lining the sides with brick or concrete and the bottom with tightly packed broken bricks and lumpy chalk, or something similar, to a depth of about a foot (30 cm.). The bed should then be filled in with loam or good garden soil mixed with mortar rubble and a small quantity of bonemeal to induce sturdy, short, jointed growths. Alternatively, a fig can be planted in paving or a hard gravel path.

A young pot-grown plant is best planted in early March. It is turned out of the pot and the roots disentangled and spread out evenly in the hole prepared for it. The soil should then be returned and firmed in the usual way.

If more than one fig is planted, allow 18 to 20 feet (6 m.) between the trees.

Pruning and Training

No pruning is necessary the first year, but new growths are trained roughly fanwise to the wall as they extend. In subsequent years young growth is stopped at the fifth leaf, preferably before the end of June, but no later, because an outdoor fig bears fruit on the tips of well-ripened shoots of the previous summer's growth (see p. 110). Stopping should not be practised unless the shoots have time to 'break' and develop other shoots which can ripen before leaf-fall. In July shoots should be tied in to the wall, giving each shoot plenty of room to develop and ripen.

Winter pruning should be delayed until March, because in a severe winter some frost damage may be expected. In cold districts, the branches are untied and bundled up in straw for the winter to prevent frost damage. The first

A concrete trough to restrict root growth of a fig tree.

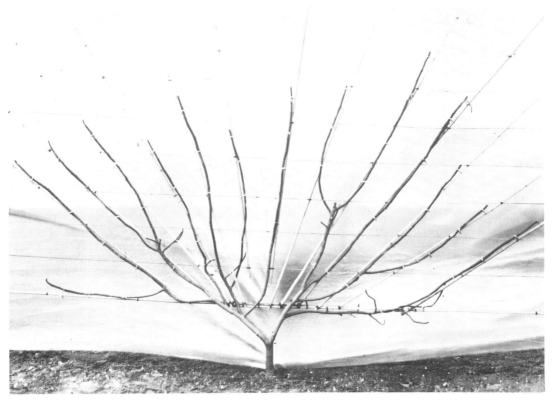

Above: A young fan-trained fig.

Right: Diagram of a fig shoot in August. A = *next years fruits;* B = *fruits which will not mature before the frosts;* C = *ripening fruits.*

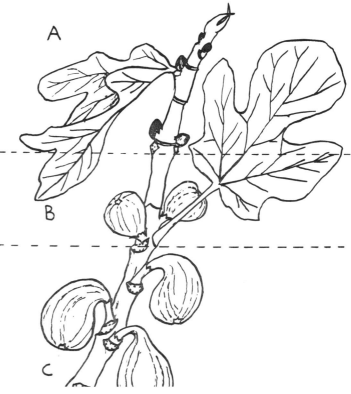

task should be to cut out all diseased or frost-damaged wood, and much of the weak wood which crosses the main branches, leaving a sufficient number of the best young growths, with ripened and undamaged tips, to cover the wall area. At that season healthy tips will already show the swelling buds of embryo figs which will mature as ripe fruits in August and September.

If desired the fan can be built up on much the same lines as for the peach (pp. 97–98).

Manuring

Over-vigorous root growth must not be encouraged and no manuring will usually be needed in the first years. But in a dry year, when the tree is carrying a heavy crop,

Tying in shoots in the summer.

both feeding and watering will be beneficial. A light mulch of rotted manure may then be applied.

Cultivation

Unless growth has been restricted as suggested on p. 109, root pruning will be necessary from time to time (see pp. 112–113).

Figs are susceptible to cold and in hard winters the branches bearing the embryo figs at their tips will require protection by straw, canvas, hurdles thatched with straw, etc.

Recommended varieties

White Marseilles, *early*
Brown Turkey, *mid-season*
Bourjasotte Grise, *late*

Diseases

CORAL SPOT shows as numerous coral-red spots on old and dead wood and can cause die-back of branches. Cut out and burn the affected branches to a point well below the diseased tissues and paint all the wounds with a protective paint.

TREATMENT OF OVER-VIGOROUS UNPRODUCTIVE TREES

Before deciding the method to be used to check the growth of over-vigorous trees some of the more usual reasons why the trees are vigorous or unproductive or both should be considered.

The trees may have been grafted onto very vigorous root-stocks. Provided there is room and the cultural conditions are right this is not a mistake as such trees will usually bear heavier crops than the same cultivar on a dwarfing or semi-dwarfing root-stock. However, they will be much later coming into bearing than the more precocious, less vigorous rootstocks.

The trees may be over-vigorous and unproductive be-cause they have been pruned too hard in the past. The effect of hard pruning is to cause most of the buds that remain to grow out as shoots instead of developing into fruit buds. Tree growth is strong but the crops are small. No pruning at all results in too many fruit buds and poor shoot growth. The aim in pruning should be to maintain a balance between fruit-fulness and vigour.

Another common fault is the application of too much nitrogen. Trees so treated make lush growth but few fruit buds and the fruits that are produced are usually large and of poor keeping quality (see page 10).

It is possible to check growth in various ways. Lighter pruning in the winter and summer pruning (p. 62) are examples.

Another method is to grow the trees in grass, which competes for nutrients and water. Where the trees may be receiving too much nitrogen, nitrogenous manures should be reduced or cut out altogether.

Other more drastic ways of reducing vigour are root pruning and bark ringing. Both have their disadvantages and bark ringing in particular should only be used when other methods have failed. Unskilful bark ringing can kill the trees. It should not be done to stone fruits because of the risk of silver leaf infection.

There are many other reasons for unfruitfulness, not always associated with excess vigour. Examples are poor pollination, starvation, bullfinch damage, frost damage, and lack of sunlight due to over-crowding or shading by taller plants or buildings.

Root pruning
Fruit trees that are producing poor crops either because they have

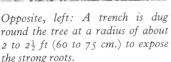

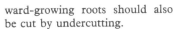

Opposite, left: A trench is dug round the tree at a radius of about 2 to 2½ ft (60 to 75 cm.) to expose the strong roots.

Above, left: The strong roots are cut and enough soil removed to enable the tree to be lifted.

Above, centre: Downward growing roots are then severed, and the fibrous ones preserved.

Above, right: The tree is replaced in the hole and the fibrous roots carefully spread out. The soil is returned to the trench, firmed down and the tree staked.

been neglected or are growing too vigorously can be induced to form fruit buds by root pruning. This is done in the winter (November/December) and means exposing and cutting back the thick anchorage roots. The thin fibrous feeding roots are left as undamaged as possible. A trench about 2 to 2½ feet (70 cm.) radius is dug round the tree and the thick roots exposed are cut. Vigorous down-ward-growing roots should also be cut by undercutting.

Young trees can be lifted to make sure all the thick roots are cut and replanted. Older trees too large to lift, have the roots cut *in situ*. With older trees, it is often better to root prune in two stages, doing one half one winter and the other half the next.

When refilling the hole firm the soil well. Root pruned trees need to be staked after the operation, and in dry spells in the following summer need to be watered copiously. It will also help to mulch a young tree with well-rotted manure or compost, keeping the mulch away from the trunk.

Bark ringing
This is another method which can

Over-vigorous trees that are too big to lift are root pruned in position. A trench is taken out round the tree at 2 to 4 ft (60 to 180 cm.) from the main stem.

113

Above, left: The smaller roots are tied back and the thick ones sawn off. Above, centre: The soil is replaced and trodden down firmly. Above, right: The roots that were tied back are untied and all the soil gradually replaced and firmed down. Below, left: A ring of bark is cut out round the main stem, by making two complete rings about $\frac{1}{4}$ in. (5 mm.) apart and removing the central strip. Below, right: The cut is covered with adhesive tape to prevent drying out and the entry of disease.

be used to bring over-vigorous trees into cropping, but it is only suitable for apples and pears. It is easier and quicker than root pruning, but can seriously damage, or kill, the tree if done incorrectly. Ringing is done at blossom time. A complete ring of bark down to the hardwood is removed from the trunk or a branch, thus disrupting part of the vascular system. As a result carbohydrates and other carbon assimilates accumulate above the wound so inducing better fruit set.

The width of the ring is determined by the age, size and vigour of the tree; the younger and smaller the tree the narrower the ring. On larger trees it should never be more than $\frac{1}{2}$ in. (12.7 mm.) wide. With a sharp knife make two parallel cuts round the trunk, cutting through the bark and soft tissue below. Peel off the bark and soft tissue and cover the ring immediately with several turns of adhesive tape. The tape must be wide enough to bridge the gap and not fall on the wound beneath. The tape can be removed when callusing is complete, in the autumn.

THE NEGLECTED FRUIT GARDEN

Renovation of Soft Fruits

Those taking over a neglected garden may find it better in the long run to uproot and burn all soft fruits, as in many cases they are unproductive due to being infected with incurable virus diseases. It is unwise to replant fruit in the same position as before. It is better to select a fresh area not previously used for fruit. After thoroughly preparing the ground, plant as suggested earlier with healthy young plants and canes. These should be acquired from a reliable source, preferably carrying the Ministry of Agriculture's certificate of virus-tested stock.

With bush fruits that have not been neglected for too long, it may be possible to rejuvenate them by cutting out old and useless wood and applying mulches, manures and fertilisers.

Ground which has been allowed to become overgrown with weeds will need to be thoroughly dug over and cleaned. This is an opportunity to incorporate organic manures, compost, or artificials suitable for the respective fruits. As far as possible avoid damage to the roots whilst digging.

Renovation of Top Fruits

Most amateurs will be loath to part with fruit trees, which have a relatively long life, but here again

Right, above: Branch of a neglected tree before pruning.
Right: The same branch after thinning out.

it will be good policy to grub up any which are too close to their neighbours, or badly diseased, or occupy too much room.

With trees that are worth retaining, first remove all dead and diseased branches. If they have not been pruned for a considerable time, there will almost certainly be too many large branches, especially in the centre of the tree. These must be removed altogether leaving the remainder well spaced out, about

2 to 3 feet (60 to 90 cm.) apart. Cut out or shorten any smaller branches that are crossing or awkwardly placed.

Apples and pears will generally need more thinning out than plums. Remember that in order to reduce the risk of infection from silver leaf disease plums should not be pruned in winter.

On apple and pear trees that are too tall, shorten some of the tallest branches. Pare down saw cuts with a sharp knife and cover

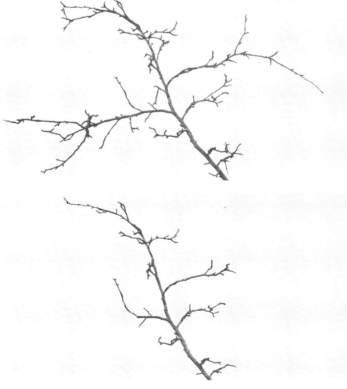

Left, above: An old apple tree that has been neglected and become overcrowded.

Left, below: The same tree after thinning out.

Right, above: An apple growing in grass and making poor growth.

Right, below: The same tree with the grass and weeds removed by hand or weedkiller and a mulch applied.

large wounds with a bituminous tree paint.

If the trees are stunted, cutting back will do little harm; but, if they are still making good or moderate growth, the thinning operation should be spread out over two or three years.

Where spur systems are congested they should be thinned out (see p. 63).

After pruning is completed, spray the tree with a winter wash in December or January.

The possibility of changing over unsuitable cultivars to desirable sorts by frame-working or top grafting can also be considered.

Weed-infested ground should be thoroughly cleaned up. With trees in grass it will be a good plan to clear the soil at the base of the trunk within a radius of some 4 feet (1.2 m.), by an application of paraquat or by a light forking. Mulches of straw or farmyard manure around the tree bases are more effective than drastic pruning in encouraging tree growth.

Pollination and subsequent fertilisation are essential processes for the production of good crops of fruit. Pollination is simply the transfer of pollen grains to the stigma of a flower and in tree fruits is mainly the work of bees and other insects.

Many of the important tree fruits are self-incompatible, which means cross-pollination is necessary if they are to set good crops. Some are self-fertile, for example peaches, nectarines and certain plums and gages, but even with these, cropping is improved if cross-pollination is provided. Cross-pollination in this context means the transfer of pollen from the flower of one cultivar to that of a different cultivar, but of the same kind of fruit.

Apples

All apples show some degree of self-incompatibility; some set no fruit at all when self-pollinated, others can set a fair crop under favourable conditions. Cropping is, however, much more satisfactory and consistent when provision is made for cross-pollination. Most are diploid, though some are triploid. Triploids are poor pollinators and where these are grown, two diploid cultivars should be planted to provide cross-pollination for the triploid and each other.

In the table on page 119 cultivars are divided into seven groups according to the flowering season. In selecting cultivars to pollinate each other, cultivars should be selected from within the same group where possible. Cultivars may be selected from the preceding or following group and their flowering periods should overlap sufficiently for cross-pollination to take place with the exception of Group 7. 'Crawley Beauty' (culinary) usually flowers when the flowering stage of all other cultivars is over and sets an adequate crop on its own. A few apples are cross-incompatible and these are listed in the Notes to the tables.

Whilst in most seasons and districts flowering will follow a regular sequence, variations will occur from year to year and also from district to district. It is known that cultivars react differently to winter temperatures and this may well cause some cultivars to flower earlier than others in some seasons and later, or at the same time, in others; in the same way variation may occur between cultivars growing in the eastern part of England compared with those in the western area in the same year.

Pears

Cultivars of pears are less self-compatible than apples and very few fruits are produced from self-pollination. 'Conference', though sometimes reported as self-fertile, is in fact self-incompatible, or nearly so. It may set parthenocarpic (seedless) fruits some of which are normal in shape, and this may account for earlier reports that 'Conference' is self-fertile.

However, parthenocarpy does not always occur and such fruits are often misshapen and of poor quality. The majority of pear cultivars are diploid, though a few are triploid or even tetraploid. Triploid cultivars behave in the same way as triploid apples and should have two cultivars as pollinators to pollinate both the triploid cultivars and each other. Two cultivars are tetraploids; 'Improved Fertility' is self-fertile, but a sport of 'Williams' known as 'Double Williams' is self-incompatible.

Two incompatibility groups are known in pears. Cultivars in these groups are all self- and cross-incompatible, that is, they will neither set fruit with their own pollen nor with the pollen of any cultivar within the same group. These are:

GROUP 1
Fondante d'Automne, Laxton's Progress, Laxton's Superb, Louise Bonne of Jersey, Précoce de Trévoux, Seckle, Williams' Bon Chrétien.

GROUP 2
Beurré d'Amanlis, Conference.

Three diploid cultivars produce little good pollen and are, therefore, useless as pollinators. These are Bristol Cross, Beurré Bedford and Marguerite Marillat.

In the following tables the cultivars are divided into 4 groups according to flowering season. Where possible, select from the

TABLE 1: FLOWERING OF APPLES

Notes

(B) = Known to be biennial or irregular in flowering.
(T) = Triploid.

Colour sports usually flower at the same time as the cultivar from which they originated.

The following combinations are incompatible: Cox's Orange Pippin pollinated by Kidd's Orange Red and the reverse. Cox's Orange Pippin is ineffective on Holstein. Golden Delicious may be ineffective on Crispin (Mutsu).

Group 1: very early
Gravenstein (T)
Lord Suffield
Mank's Codlin (B)
Red Astrachan
Stark Earliest (syn.
   Scarlet Pimpernel)

Group 2
Acme
Adam's Pearmain (B)
Baker's Delicious
Beauty of Bath
Ben's Red (B)
Bismarck (B)
Cheddar Cross
Christmas Pearmain (B)
Devonshire Quarrenden (B)
Egremont Russet
George Cave
George Neal
Golden Spire
Idared
Irish Peach
Kerry Pippin
Keswick Codlin (B)
Laxton's Early Crimson
Lord Lambourne
Maidstone Favourite
Margil
McIntosh Red
Melba (B)
Merton Charm
Michaelmas Red
Norfolk Beauty
Rev. W. Wilks (B)
Ribston Pippin (T)
Ross Nonpareil
St Edmund's Pippin
Striped Beefing
Warner's King (T)
Washington (T)
White Transparent

Group 3
Allington Pippin (B)
Arthur Turner
Barnack Orange
Baumann's Reinette (B)
Belle de Boskoop (T)
Belle de Pontoise (B)
Blenheim Orange (TB)
Bowden's Seedling
Bramley's Seedling (T)
Brownlee's Russet
Charles Ross
Chivers Delight
Cox's Orange Pippin
Crispin (T)
D'Arcy Spice
Discovery
Duchess Favourite
Emperor Alexander
Emneth Early (Early
   Victoria) (B)
Epicure
Exeter Cross
Exquisite
Feltham Beauty
Fortune (B)
Granny Smith
Greensleeves
Grenadier
Hambling's Seedling
Holstein (T)
Hormead Pearmain
James Grieve
John Standish
Jonathan
Katja
Kidd's Orange Red
King of Tompkins
   County (T)
Langley Pippin
Loddington (Stone's)
Lord Grosvenor
Lord Hindlip
Malling Kent
Mère de Ménage
Merton Knave
Merton Prolific

Merton Russet
Merton Worcester
Miller's Seedling (B)
New Hawthornden
Ontario
Peasgood's Nonsuch
Queen
Red Victoria (B)
Reinette du Canada (T)
Rival (B)
Rosemary Russet
St Cecilia
St Everard
Spartan
Stirling Castle
Sturmer Pippin
Sunset
Taunton Cross
Tom Putt
Tydeman's Early
   Worcester
Wagener (B)
Wealthy
Worcester Pearmain
S.T. Wright
Wyken Pippin

Group 4
Annie Elizabeth
Ashmead's Kernel
Autumn Pearmain
Cellini
Claygate Pearmain
Cornish Gillyflower
Cox's Pomona
Delicious
Duke of Devonshire
Dumelow's Seedling
   (Wellington)
Ellison's Orange
Encore
Gala
George Carpenter
Gladstone (B)
Golden Delicious
Golden Noble
Hawthornden

Herring's Pippin
Howgate Wonder
Ingrid Marie
Joybells
King's Acre Pippin
Lady Henniker
Lady Sudeley
Lane's Prince Albert
Laxton's Pearmain
Lord Derby
Mannington's Pearmain
Merton Joy
Monarch (B)
Orleans Reinette
Pixie
Sir John Thornycroft
Superb (Laxton's) (B)
Tydeman's Late Orange
Woolbrook Russet
Yellow Newtown (B)

Group 5
Coronation (B)
Frogmore Prolific (B)
Gascoyne's Scarlet (T)
Heusgen's Golden
   Reinette
King of the Pippins (B)
Merton Beauty
Mother (American)
Newtown Wonder
Northern Spy (B)
Reinette Rouge Etoilée
Royal Jubilee
Suntan (T)
William Crump
Winston
Woolbrook Pippin (B)

Group 6
Bess Pool
Court Pendu Plat
Edward VII
Laxton's Royalty

Group 7: very late
Crawley Beauty

TABLE 2: FLOWERING OF PEARS

Notes
(T) = Triploid.
(M.S.) = Male sterile (ineffective as a pollinator).

Group 1: very early	Louise Bonne of Jersey	Durondeau	Group 4: late
Brockworth Park	Marguerite Marillat (M.S.)	Fertility	Beurré Bedford (M.S.)
Maréchal de la Cour (T)	Packham's Triumph	Fondante d'Automne	Beurré Mortillet
Précoce de Trévoux	Passe Crasanne	Fondante Thirriott	Bristol Cross (M.S.)
	Princess	Hessle	Calebasse Bosc
Group 2	Seckle	Jargonelle (T)	Catillac (T)
Baronne de Mello	St Luke	Joséphine de Malines	Clapp's Favourite
Bellissime d'Hiver	Uvedale's St Germain (T)	Laxton's Early Market	Doyenné du Comice
Beurré Alexandre Lucas	Vicar of Winkfield (T)	Laxton's Progress	Glou Morceau
(T)		Laxton's Satisfaction	Gorham
Beurré d'Amanlis (T)	**Group 3**	Le Lectier	Improved Fertility
Beurré d'Anjou	Belle-Julie	Merton Pride (T)	Laxton's Foremost
Beurré Clairgeau	Beurré Dumont	Nouvelle Fulvie	Laxton's Victor
Beurré Diel (T)	Beurré Hardy	Olivier de Serres	Marie Louise
Beurré Giffard	Beurré Superfin	Roosevelt	Napoleon
Beurré Six	Black Worcester	Souvenir du Congrés	Nouveau Poiteau
Comtesse de Paris	Conference	Thompson's	Onward
Doyenné d'Été	Doyenné Boussoch (T)	Triomphe de Vienne	Pitmaston Duchess (T)
Duchesse d'Angouléme	Doyenné George Boucher	Williams' Bon Chrétien	Santa Claus
Easter Beurré	Dr Jules Guyot		Winter Nelis
Emile d'Heyst	Duchesse de Bordeaux		Zépherin Grégoire

same flowering group when choosing cultivars for mutual cross-pollination, though in many cases the flowering period of cultivars in adjacent groups will provide sufficient overlap.

Plums
The myrobalan or cherry plums are diploids and are self-compatible. Most other plums, damsons and bullaces grown in this country are hexaploids and may be completely self-compatible, partly self-compatible or completely self-incompatible. All except the completely self-compatible cultivars require inter-planted pollinators to set fruits. Cross-incompatibility also occurs, three groups being known.

In a protracted flowering season the time of start of full bloom from the earliest cultivar to the latest is about 20 days. In the table shown opposite this has been divided into four-day periods and the cultivars divided accordingly into five flowering groups. When selecting pollinators for cultivars which occur in either compatibility Group A or B, the choice

is preferably restricted to those whose flowering group is the same as or adjacent to, that of the cultivar to be cross-pollinated. A pollinator may be selected from any of the three compatibility groups.

Groups of incompatible plums
GROUP I
Jefferson
Coe's Golden Drop
Allgrove's Superb
Coe's Violet Gage
Crimson Drop

GROUP II
President
Late Orange
Old Greengage*
Cambridge Gage

GROUP III
Early Rivers
Blue Rock

* Four cultivars, perhaps bud sports, are distributed as Old Greengage. They are all in Group II. The differences are mainly in flower and leaf characters.

IN GROUP I
All pollinations fail.

IN GROUP II
Late Orange × President fails both ways.
Late Orange or President pollinated by Cambridge Gage or Old Greengage set a full crop.
Cambridge Gage or Old Greengage pollinated by Late Orange or President set only 2 per cent.

IN GROUP III
Early Rivers pollinated by Blue Rock sets a full crop.
Blue Rock pollinated by Early Rivers sets a very poor crop.

Cherries
Most sweet cherries are not only completely self-incompatible, but cross-incompatibility between groups also exists. This means that none of the older cultivars of sweet cherry will set fruit with its own pollen nor with the pollen of any variety within its own incompatibility group, but will set fruit when pollinated by any variety in another group provided they flower at the same time. The only

TABLE 3: FLOWERING OF PLUMS

Compatibility Group A Self-incompatible	Compatibility Group B Partly self-compatible	Compatibility Group C Self-compatible	Unclassified
Flowering Group 1: Early			
Black Prince	Angelina Burdett	Monarch	Olympia
Grand Duke	Blue Rock		
Heron	Utility		
Jefferson			
Late Orleans			
Mallard			
Flowering Group 2			
Admiral	Ariel	Brahy's Greengage	
Black Diamond	Curlew	Brandy Gage	
Coe's Crimson Drop		Denniston's Superb	
Coe's Golden Drop		Goliath	
Coe's Violet		Guthrie's Late	
President		Prosperity	
		Reine-Claude de Bavay	
		Warwickshire Drooper	
Flowering Group 3			
Allgrove's Superb	Belgian Purple	Aylesbury Prune	Archduke
Bryanston Gage	Cox's Emperor	Bastard Victoria	Laxton's Abundance
Late Orange	Early Laxton	Bonne de Bry	Swan
Washington	Early Rivers	Bountiful	Wye Cross
	Goldfinch	Czar	
	Merton Gem	Edwards	
	Reine-Claude Violette	Golden Transparent	
	Thames Cross	Laxton's Cropper	
		Laxton's Gage	
		Laxton's Supreme	
		Merryweather Damson	
		Opal	
		Pershore	
		Purple Pershore	
		Severn Cross	
		Victoria	
Flowering Group 4			
Count Althann's Gage	Cambridge Gage	Blaisdon Red	
Kirke's	Farleigh Damson	Bradley's King Damson	
Peach	Stint	Early Transparent Gage	
Wyedale		Giant Prune	
		Ontario	
		Oullins Golden Gage	
Flowering Group 5			
Delicious		Belle de Louvain	Pacific
Frogmore Damson		Belle de Septembre	Teme Cross
Late Transparent		Gisborne's	
Old Greengage		Kentish Bush	
Pond's Seedling		Laxton's Blue Tit	
Red Magnum Bonum		Marjorie's Seedling	
		Shropshire Damson	

TABLE 4: FLOWERING OF ACID AND DUKE CHERRIES

Notes

S.C. = Self-compatible.
P.S.C. = Partly self-compatible (setting only a light crop when selfed).
S.I. = Self-incompatible.
* Kentish Red exists in two forms under this name; one is self-incompatible and the other is self-compatible.

Capable of pollinating sweet cherries in Groups below	Cultivar	Degree of compatibility	Picking season
	Duke cherries		
Group 3	May Duke	P.S.C.	Early mid-season
	Royal Duke	P.S.C.	Late mid-season
Group 4	Archduke	P.S.C.	Late mid-season
Group 5	Belle de Chatenay	S.I.	Very late
Group 6	Ronald's Late Duke	S.C.	Very late
	Acid cherries		
Group 4	Kentish Red*	S.I. or S.C.	Mid-season
	Wye Morello	S.C.	Late
Group 5	Montmorency	S.C.	Late
	Morello	S.C.	Late
	Flemish Red	S.C.	Late

exception to self-incompatibility is found in the last group shown in the table after group 13, represented by the Canadian cultivar 'Stella'.

The groups are indicated in the following table.

The sour and duke cherries, unlike the diploid sweet cherries, are tetraploids. Some are self-fertile, others are self-incompatible and require cross-pollination, but there are no known cases of cross-incompatibility in the sour and duke cherries. Sweet cherries are not suitable pollinators for sour or duke cherries, which however, are capable of pollinating sweet cherries although most of them flower rather too late to be very useful.

The cultivars are arranged in groups so that any cultivar in one of the flowering groups will flower sufficiently close to any other in the same group, or in the group either directly preceding, or immediately following it; for example, the ideal pollinators for 'Roundel' will be found within the same flowering group (group 3), but it could also be pollinated by any cultivar in flowering groups 2 or 4, provided the variety chosen is not in the same incompatibility group as 'Roundel'. Thus 'Merton Heart' in flowering group 2, 'Elton Heart' in flowering group 3 or 'Emperor Francis' in flowering group 4 will be found satisfactory.

TABLE 5: FLOWERING OF SWEET CHERRIES

Notes

Season of ripening: (E) = early; (EM) = early mid-season; (M) = mid-season; (LM) = late mid-season; (L) = late; (VL) = very late.
Cultivars available under the EMLA scheme are in *italics*.
*Group O are universal donors.

Incompatibility Groups	Flowering period 1 (Earliest)	Flowering period 2	Flowering period 3	Flowering period 4	Flowering period 5	Flowering period 6 (Latest)
Group O * Groups	Noir de Guben (LM) Nutberry Black (EM)			Smoky Dun (M)	Bigarreau Gaucher (L) Florence (L)	
Group 1	Early Rivers (E)	Bedford Prolific (EM) Black Circassian (EM) Knights Early Black (EM)	Roundel (M)			
Group 2		Bigarreau de Schrecken (EM) Merton Favourite (EM) Waterloo (M)	Frogmore Early (EM) Merton Bigarreau (M) Merton Bounty (EM) Van (LM)	Belle Agathe (VL) Merton Crane (M)	Black Elton (M)	
Group 3			Merton Marvel (LM)	Emperor Francis (LM) Napoleon (LM) Ohio Beauty (L)		
Group 4			Merton Premier (EM)	Kent Bigarreau (LM)		
Group 5					Late Black Bigarreau (LM)	
Group 6	Werder's Early Black (E)	Merton Heart (EM)	Early Amber (EM) Elton Heart (M) Governor Wood (EM)			
Group 7				Bigarreau Hâtif Burlat (E)	Hooker's Black (LM)	Bradbourne Black (LM) Géante d'Hedelfinger (LM)
Group 8			Peggy Rivers (EM)			
Group 9				Merton Reward (M)	Merton Late (VL)	
Group 12						Noble (L)
Group 13			Vic (LM)			
Self Compatible				Stella (LM)		

A brief outline of the various tasks which should be done is given on this page. For full details of each operation turn to the chapter dealing with the fruit crop in question.

The timing of spray application for control of pests and diseases is based on the stages of bud development. Dates for these stages can only be approximate because the rate of growth will vary according to locality and season. For full details of each control see the paragraphs headed Pests and Diseases *in the chapter on the fruit concerned.*

For full details of herbicides mentioned see pages 15–16.

Inspect fruits in store and remove any that are rotten.

Continue planting when soil conditions are right.

Select and heel-in scionwood in a cold, sheltered, shaded position for grafting later.

Apply potash to strawberries, gooseberries, red and white currants.

Check all tree stakes and ties, and make sure they are firm and sound.

Continue pruning of apples and pears except in hard frost. Collect and burn the prunings. Prune newly planted cane fruits. Continue pruning established and newly planted bush fruits.

Pests and diseases

Spray dormant fruit trees, canes and bushes with tar oil, to control overwintering aphid and sucker eggs – if this was not done in December.

Inspect apples and pears for canker and treat where necessary.

Spray peaches and nectarines against peach leaf curl. Repeat in 10 to 14 days.

The effect of severe bird damage to plum trees. Much of the wood becomes bare and unproductive.

A brief outline of the various tasks which should be done is given on this page. For full details of each operation turn to the chapter dealing with the fruit crop in question.

The timing of spray application for control of pests and diseases is based on the stages of bud development. Dates for these stages can only be approximate because the rate of growth will vary according to locality and season. For full details of each control see the paragraphs headed Pests and Diseases *in the chapter on the fruit concerned.*

For full details of herbicides mentioned see pages 15–16.

Inspect fruits in store and remove any that are rotten.

Continue planting fruit trees and bushes when soil conditions are right.

Apply simazine to established fruit trees and bushes.

Apply potash to apples, pears and plums. Apply nitrogen in early February to trees in grass, and in late February to those in cultivated land.

Mulch young trees, bushes and cane fruits with manure or compost.

Prune newly planted and established stone fruits (except pyramid plums – see April) as growth begins in late February.

Complete the formative pruning of newly-planted apples and pears, and continue pruning the older trees except in hard frost.

Prune established autumn fruiting raspberries. Tip summer fruiting raspberries. If not already done, cut down newly-planted canes to 9 to 12 inches (23–30 cm.).

Cover strawberries for an early crop with polythene tunnels or glass cloches early in the month.

Untie young canes of blackberries

and related fruits which have been bundled together against winter damage. Train onto the wires before bud burst.

Protect the blossom on wall-trained trees by draping with hessian, double thickness netting, etc. whenever frost is expected. Hand pollinate if flowering is early and insects scarce.

Pests and diseases

Complete tar oil spraying on

apples and pears. As an alternative to tar oil use DNOC-petroleum wash on apples in late February if there is evidence of heavy infestation of red spider mite.

Spray peaches and nectarines against peach leaf curl. Repeat in 10 to 14 days.

Inspect apple and pear trees for canker and treat if necessary. Spray severely infected trees. Protect all large pruning cuts.

Polythene tunnel for strawberries, showing the method of tying.

MARCH : WORK IN THE FRUIT GARDEN

A brief outline of the various tasks which should be done is given on this page. For full details of each operation turn to the chapter dealing with the fruit crop in question.

The timing of spray application for control of pests and diseases is based on the stages of bud development. Dates for these stages can only be approximate because the rate of growth will vary according to locality and season. For full details of each control see the paragraphs headed Pests and Diseases *in the chapter on the fruit concerned.*

For full details of herbicides mentioned see pages 15–16.

Finish all planting and pruning of trees and bushes, early in the month.

Apply potash to cane fruits.

Complete mulching young trees, bushes and cane fruits.

Apply nitrogen to black currants.

Apply simazine or dichlobenil to established fruit trees and bushes. Paraquat can also be used to kill annual weeds and shallow-rooted perennials.

Give a second application of nitrogen to pears in grass.

Cleft graft apples, pears and plums.

Protect the blossom on wall-trained trees when frost is forecast. Hand pollinate if flowers are early and insects are scarce.

Untie and retrain branches of wall-trained figs, bundled together for protection. Prune as necessary.

On established acid cherries prune out a proportion of older wood.

Untie and retrain canes of blackberries, and related fruits.

Plant strawberry runners.

Pests and diseases
If a winter wash has been applied control of aphid, sucker and scale insects may not be necessary, but if aphids are present spray with a systemic insecticide.

Spray apples against scab at bud burst and again at green cluster. Spray against aphids, apple sucker, capsid and caterpillars.

Spray pears against scab at bud burst, green bud and white bud (10 to 14 day intervals). Control aphids and caterpillars, and if necessary pear midge and pear leaf blister mite.

Spray plums, cherries and damsons against aphids and caterpillars at bud burst to white bud.

Spray black currants against gall mite (big bud) at the late grape stage and repeat after 3 weeks. Spray against aphids if present.

Spray gooseberries against gooseberry mildew just before the flowers open; repeat at fruit set and 14 days later.

Spray cane fruits against spur blight and cane spot, at bud burst, and against aphids if necessary.

Right, above: Bud-burst of apple.
Right: Grape stage of black currant.

A brief outline of the various tasks which should be done is given on this page. For full details of each operation turn to the chapter dealing with the fruit crop in question.

The timing of spray application for control of pests and diseases is based on the stages of bud development. Dates for these stages can only be approximate because the rate of growth will vary according to locality and season. For full details of each control see the paragraphs headed Pests and Diseases *in the chapter on the fruit concerned.*

For full details of herbicides mentioned see pages 15–16.

Early flowering fruits may need some protection from frost by covering with hessian, double thickness nylon or fish netting or similar materials whenever frost is imminent. Uncover immediately afterwards so that pollination is not impeded.

Ventilate protected strawberries on sunny days. If growth is poor apply a light dressing of nitrogen. Finish planting runners by mid-April. De-blossom spring-planted summer-fruiting strawberries in their first year.

Prune gooseberries, red and white currants left unpruned during the winter owing to the likelihood of bird damage.

Prune pyramid plums in their early years.

Spray wall-trained peach and nectarine flowers at mid-day with a fine mist to help setting in dry conditions.

Finish planting raspberries and cut back the newly-planted canes. Check on netting for bird protection and prepare supports.

Graft top fruits, using whip and tongue graft (see p. 53). Top-working top fruits to change the cultivar can also be done this month.

Pests and diseases

Do not use insecticides during flowering of any crop as bees and other pollinating insects will be killed.

Continue scab control on apples and if not already done, control aphids, apple sucker, capsid, caterpillars and woolly aphids before open blossom. Start spraying against mildew at green cluster if using thiophanate-methyl or benomyl, or at pink bud if using dinocap.

Continue with scab control on pears (white bud to full bloom); also control aphids and caterpillars, and, if necessary, pear midge and pear leaf blister mite before open blossom.

Spray peaches and nectarines at petal-fall against red spider mite and aphids.

Control sawfly on plums at cot split (about 8 days after flowering) if necessary.

Control aphids and caterpillars on cherries before open blossom.

Apply the second spray to black currants against gall mite. Spray for aphids if present. Start spraying against leaf spot.

Continue control of gooseberry mildew on gooseberries. Control gooseberry sawfly. Start spraying against leaf spot, if necessary.

Inspect strawberries for aphids and spray if necessary. Spray at first open flower against grey mould (botrytis) on plants under glass or polythene (but do not use dichlofluanid).

Spray raspberries against spur blight if necessary.

Further development of apple buds. Right, above: Green cluster. Right: Pink bud.

A brief outline of the various tasks which should be done is given on this page. For full details of each operation turn to the chapter dealing with the fruit crop in question.

The timing of spray application for control of pests and diseases is based on the stages of bud development. Dates for these stages can only be approximate because the rate of growth will vary according to locality and season. For full details of each control see the paragraphs headed Pests and Diseases *in the chapter on the fruit concerned.*

For full details of herbicides mentioned see pages 15–16.

Pick protected strawberries and gooseberry thinnings.

Open one side of fruit cage to allow easier access of pollinating insects.

Protect blossoms from frost, when necessary. Keep the grass short.

Ensure no fruit suffers from lack of water after flowering, particularly wall-trained stone fruits.

Bark-ring over-vigorous apple and pear trees.

De-blossom newly-planted fruit trees.

Start deshooting wall-trained peaches and nectarines, with some light thinning.

On wall-trained plums and damsons remove shoots growing directly towards or out from the wall.

Shorten leaders of all mature trees grown in a restricted form.

De-blossom spring-planted runners of summer-fruiting strawberries. Clean up weeds before strawing. Continue to ventilate protected plants on sunny days. Net against birds. Remove flowers formed on perpetuals.

Control weeds in soft fruits by hoeing or herbicides.

Pull out unwanted shoots of raspberries causing overcrowding or growing between the rows.

Thin gooseberries in late May if large dessert fruits are required.

Pests and diseases
Never apply insecticides during flowering as they will kill bees and other pollinating insects.

Control apple sawfly and capsid at petal-fall, also red spider mite if present. Continue scab and mildew control.

Spray against pear scab at petal-fall and repeat as necessary.

Control sawfly on plums at cot split, if necessary.

Continue leaf spot control on currants and start control of gooseberry mildew if necessary.

Spray gooseberries against mildew and leaf spot. Control sawfly caterpillars if present.

Spray raspberries before flowering against cane spot and spur blight. Spray against grey mould.

Spray blackberries, etc. against cane spot in mid-May, and against spur blight if necessary.

Spray or dust strawberries immediately before flowering against mildew; repeat 10 to 14 days later. When the first flowers open spray against grey mould. Control slugs if present.

Stages for spraying apples. Left: Petal fall. Right: Fruitlet stage.

A brief outline of the various tasks which should be done is given on this page. For full details of each operation turn to the chapter dealing with the fruit crop in question.

The timing of spray application for control of pests and diseases is based on the stages of bud development. Dates for these stages can only be approximate because the rate of growth will vary according to locality and season. For full details of each control see the paragraphs headed Pests and Diseases *in the chapter on the fruit concerned.*

For full details of herbicides mentioned see pages 15–16.

Pick strawberries, raspberries, red and white currants, gooseberries and cherries.

Irrigate tree, bush and cane fruits as necessary.

Keep the grass short, and weeds under control.

Continue disbudding on wall-trained peaches and nectarines and tie in selected shoots. Thin fruits.

Thin plum fruits. In two stages, first in early June and finally in late June.

Continue removing shoots from fan-trained cherries and plums, that are growing directly towards or out from the wall. Pinch back other laterals and tie in.

If set of apples is heavy, thin lightly. Wait until after the 'June drop' for the final thinning.

Thin pears if fruit set is heavy.

Pinch out tip buds on young shoots of mature figs at 5 leaves.

Net soft fruits against birds.

Straw down strawberries (or use black polythene or mats). Ventilate protected strawberries. Remove cloches and tunnels when fruiting finished. Peg down runners for new plants, otherwise remove them.

Continue to select raspberry shoots and loosely tie in. On newly-planted plants prune down old canes once new shoots are produced.

Train new shoots of blackberries, etc.

Thin gooseberries and use thinnings for cooking. Summer prune at end of June.

Summer prune bush and cordon red and white currants at the end of June.

Pests and diseases
Continue to spray apples regularly against scab and mildew. Inspect for red spider mite and spray if present. Spray against codling moth about mid-June and again 3 weeks later. Spray against bitter pit in mid-June if necessary.

Inspect stone fruits for red spider mites and aphids and spray if present.

Continue leafspot and gooseberry mildew control on currants.

Inspect gooseberries for caterpillars of gooseberry sawfly and magpie moth and control if present. Spray once or twice against leaf spot after harvest if necessary.

Control grey mould and mildew on strawberries. Control slugs if present.

Spray cane fruits against spur blight and cane spot immediately before flowering and against grey mould as the first flowers open. Spray against raspberry beetle when most blossom is over and again after 14 days.

Gooseberries ready for picking.

A brief outline of the various tasks which should be done is given on this page. For full details of each operation turn to the chapter dealing with the fruit crop in question.

The timing of spray application for control of pests and diseases is based on the stages of bud development. Dates for these stages can only be approximate because the rate of growth will vary according to locality and season. For full details of each control see the paragraphs headed Pests and Diseases *in the chapter on the fruit concerned.*

For full details of herbicides mentioned see pages 15–16.

Pick strawberries, gooseberries, currants, blackberries, raspberries, cherries and peaches.

Check trees for tie constriction.

Complete thinning of apples. Support heavily laden branches. Irrigate if necessary. Summer prune all trained forms.

Summer prune pears.

Prop up heavily-laden branches of plums and damsons.

Continue training of fan-trained plums and cherries.

Complete pruning of cherry trees.

Continue training of wall-trained peaches and nectarines. Protect fruits against birds.

After fruiting cut out old raspberry canes and tie in new ones. Remove unwanted suckers and control weeds.

After fruiting is over cut off the old leaves of summer-fruiting strawberries and remove straw; remove runners and weeds, burn all the debris and apply simazine for long-term weed control. Continue propagation of new plants.

Train in new canes of blackberries etc. Tip layering for new plants can be done at the end of the month.

Red currants ready for picking.

Pests and diseases
Apply a second spray to apples against codling moth caterpillars (3 weeks after the first). Continue regular sprays against mildew until mid-July. Continue spraying against bitter pit if necessary. Check whether scab is present and if necessary continue spraying until mid-July. Inspect for woolly aphid and treat if found.

Apply second spray to blackberries, etc. against raspberry beetle 14 days after the first.

On currants and gooseberries continue to control leaf spot and gooseberry mildew after harvesting.

A brief outline of the various tasks which should be done is given on this page. For full details of each operation turn to the chapter dealing with the fruit crop in question.

The timing of spray application for control of pests and diseases is based on the stages of bud development. Dates for these stages can only be approximate because the rate of growth will vary according to locality and season. For full details of each control see the paragraphs headed Pests and Diseases *in the chapter on the fruit concerned.*

For full details of herbicides mentioned see pages 15–16.

Pick strawberries, blackberries, loganberries, raspberries, gooseberries, black and red currants, figs, plums, damsons, cherries, peaches, apples and pears.

Continue pruning of restricted forms of apples and pears. Begin pruning of over-vigorous trees. Support heavily laden branches. Tie down laterals of spindlebush trees where necessary. Protect fruits against birds.

Immediately after wall-trained peaches and nectarines have fruited, cut out the shoots which have borne fruit and dead wood and tie in replacement shoots.

Prune plums and damsons after fruiting, and cut out any broken branches. Remove dead wood on fan-trained plums, shorten pinched-back shoots and tie in.

Prepare new strawberry beds and plant out rooted runners.

Apply simazine for weed control in established strawberries only.

Continue pruning and tying in of raspberries.

Continue training new canes of blackberries, etc.

Pests and diseases
On apple give last spray against bitter pit. Spray mid-August to reduce losses from brown rot in store.

Spray stone fruits after harvest but not before mid-August against bacterial canker if necessary.

Continue with leaf spot control on gooseberries and currants after harvesting, and with control of gooseberry mildew if necessary.

'Cambridge Gage' plums ready for picking.

A brief outline of the various tasks which should be done is given on this page. For full details of each operation turn to the chapter dealing with the fruit crop in question.

The timing of spray application for control of pests and diseases is based on the stages of bud development. Dates for these stages can only be approximate because the rate of growth will vary according to locality and season. For full details of each control see the paragraphs headed Pests and Diseases *in the chapter on the fruit concerned.*

For full details of herbicides mentioned see pages 15–16.

Pick strawberries (perpetual and 'Redgauntlet'), raspberries (autumn-fruiting), blackberries, plums, damsons, peaches, figs, and early and mid-season apples and pears.

Order new trees and bushes.

Complete summer pruning of apples and pears.

Prepare for fruit storage by cleaning wooden trays and boxes.

Prune plums and damsons immediately after picking.

Complete pruning of wall-trained peaches and nectarines.

Remove dead wood on wall-trained cherries, shorten pinched back shoots and complete tying in. Cut out or tie down strong vertical shoots.

Continue planting strawberries. Cover 'Redgauntlet' for a second crop.

Complete the pruning and tying-in of summer-fruiting raspberries.

Prune black currants. Take cuttings from healthy bushes.

Cut off mildewed tips of gooseberry shoots and burn. Take cuttings.

Cut off old blackberry, etc. canes after fruiting and tie in the new. In very cold districts bundle the canes together after leaf-fall and tie to one wire.

Pests and diseases
Look for canker on apple and treat. Spray in early September to check brown rot in store.

Apply a second spray to stone fruits against bacterial canker if necessary.

A dwarf pyramid apple coming into fruiting.

A brief outline of the various tasks which should be done is given on this page. For full details of each operation turn to the chapter dealing with the fruit crop in question.

The timing of spray application for control of pests and diseases is based on the stages of bud development. Dates for these stages can only be approximate because the rate of growth will vary according to locality and season. For full details of each control see the paragraphs headed Pests and Diseases *in the chapter on the fruit concerned.*

For full details of herbicides mentioned see pages 15–16.

Pick strawberries, raspberries, blackberries, plums, apples and pears.

Store fruit of sound condition. Bring down the temperature by ventilating at night. Do not mix late apples in the store with earlier cultivars, and keep apples and pears separate.

Apply dalapon round established apples and pears for couch control.

Prune black currants if not already done. Take cuttings from healthy bushes.

Prune gooseberries, red and white currants at leaf-fall (if bird damage is likely pruning can be left until spring). Take cuttings.

Finish pruning of blackberries, etc.

Cover perpetual strawberries to extend the season. Complete planting of runners by mid-October. Tidy up beds and remove old and dead leaves from perpetuals.

Order new fruit trees and bushes and start planting immediately after leaf fall. Prepare the ground for planting before the trees arrive.

Pests and diseases
Check apple trees for canker and control if necessary; spray severely affected trees just before leaf-fall.

At the end of the month, greaseband apple and cherry trees on which spraying is not feasible.

Apply final spray at leaf-fall to stone fruits against bacterial canker. Spray peaches and nectarines against peach leaf curl; this will suffice as the mid-October spray against bacterial canker.

Sheds or outhouses are usually more suitable for storing fruit than a spare room or attic. The more insulation that can be given the better and the shade of trees or hedges will help to keep the temperature down.

A brief outline of the various tasks which should be done is given on this page. For full details of each operation turn to the chapter dealing with the fruit crop in question.

The timing of spray application for control of pests and diseases is based on the stages of bud development. Dates for these stages can only be approximate because the rate of growth will vary according to locality and season. For full details of each control see the paragraphs headed Pests and Diseases *in the chapter on the fruit concerned.*

For full details of herbicides mentioned see pages 15–16.

Complete picking of all but the very late apples and pears.

Ventilate the fruit store at night to bring down the temperature.

Ensure the fruit cage is closed and the netting in good order.

Plant new trees and bushes as soon as possible, and prune after planting.

Root prune over-vigorous trees after leaf-fall.

On summer pruned apples and pears, where secondary shoots have been produced, prune back to mature wood.

Prune established apples and pears immediately after leaf-fall. Carry out the formative pruning of dwarf pyramid, espalier and fan forms of apples and pears (thereafter prune in summer). Young tip-bearing cordons or those lacking in vigour can be tipped (thereafter prune in summer).

Apply dalapon for couch control round established apples, pears, black currants, gooseberries and cane fruits.

Remove broken branches of stone fruits and protect the wounds.

A tree after planting, the trunk protected by a tree guard and the tie incorporating a cushion between stake and trunk.

Complete pruning of blackberries, etc.

Complete pruning of raspberries. Check supports and wires and ensure canes are securely tied.

Prune currants and gooseberries. Take cuttings from healthy bushes.

Weed strawberries, remove runners. Remove old and dead leaves from perpetuals.

Pests and diseases

Net or cotton all fruits (but especially gooseberries and plums) against birds where possible.

Inspect apples and pears for canker and treat: spray severely infected trees just before leaf-fall and at 50% leaf-fall.

Spray peaches and nectarines against peach leaf curl just before leaf-fall if not already done.

A brief outline of the various tasks which should be done is given on this page. For full details of each operation turn to the chapter dealing with the fruit crop in question.

The timing of spray application for control of pests and diseases is based on the stages of bud development. Dates for these stages can only be approximate because the rate of growth will vary according to locality and season. For full details of each control see the paragraphs headed Pests and Diseases *in the chapter on the fruit concerned.*

For full details of herbicides mentioned see pages 15–16.

Complete picking very late apples, before hard frosts come.

Inspect stored fruits, and remove rotten ones.

Finish any necessary root pruning.

Plant all fruits when soil conditions are suitable. If the soil is too wet loosen the bundles, remove the packing material and heel the plants in. If the soil is frozen keep the plants in a cool, frost-proof place. Ensure roots do not dry out and plant as soon as possible.

Prune apples, pears, bush and cane fruits. Continue pruning except in hard freezing conditions, dealing with the young trees first, and then the older trees. Collect the prunings and burn.

Apply simazine to established strawberries for weed control.

Untie those laterals on spindle bush apple trees which have 'set' at the required angle.

Check the condition of all stakes, supports and ties for trees. Look for and remedy wind rocking or constriction.

In cold districts loosely bundle fig branches together and cover with mats or straw to provide winter protection. Mulch the rooting area with straw or bracken.

In cold districts bundle the new canes of blackberries etc, together and tie to a wire for winter protection.

Pests and diseases
Start spraying of dormant tree, bush and cane fruits with tar oil winter wash to control aphids, sucker and scale insects. (If red spider mite has been troublesome see February.)

Complete the spraying of stone fruits by the end of the month.

Inspect apples and pears for canker and treat where necessary.

Heel in new fruit trees if they arrive when soil conditions are unsuitable for planting.

INDEX

This index is provided as a supplement to the contents page.